I Declare War

A Handbook for
Deliverance Ministers

by
Dr. Deborah W. Nelson

PRESS

Dedication

This book would be deficient without mention of my "Mother" Marion J. Harlan. The measure of her support and confidence in her children is astounding. Her prayers and constant lifting and nurturing, without a hint of doubt or criticism, made this most challenging task possible. Her rich and most inspiring words were: "Do what you love and believe in; God will do the rest." If I had my choice of "Mothers," with all respect, you would be the one I would select. As a writer once quoted: "To the world you may just be one person, but to one person you may just be the World."

Table of Contents

Deliverance Ministry

DELIVERANCE MINISTRY is a very complex ministry and one that it is very real. The world has led even the Church into the mindset that deliverance is about theatrics and gimmicks. The image of a monstrous, behorned, red-eyed animal figure attacking Christians is not consistent with the clear teachings of the Bible. This book (based on the author's research) will serve as a reference that reveals the truth against various myths about deliverance that are widespread in the Church. It will help those who are called to Deliverance Ministry understand what can be done to stop the activities of the devil in the lives of God's people. This work is not hypothetical in its nature; it is actuality confirmed by the truth of the Word of God. Scripture contains many references to deliverance.

The Church must be open to discussing these passages and applying their truth. There is no excuse for ignorance in the Body of Christ concerning spiritual matters. One of the gains and benefits of this research is to free the mind of preconceived notions about the spirit realm and encourage the Church to seek "freedom" for the people of God. Legitimate Deliverance Ministry has been harmed by many who have intentionally incited fear and paranoia in people to render the Church powerless. Knowledge is power, however, and spiritual truths should be taught and practiced from the inception of Jesus Christ as Lord and Savior in the Church. This gives the Body of Christ an accurate picture of the victory that Jesus won on the cross.

The Spirit of God is the one person who opens minds to spiritual truths. Anyone or anything that manifests out of fear in the spiritual realm is not of God and should immediately be rebuked. The only legitimate "fear" in the Kingdom of God is a reverential fear of who God really is in all His magnificent power and glory. Any information that fails to align biblically and spiritually with the Word of God is bogus. This book has stressed the importance of the Word of God as being the ultimate standard as well as the point at which Christians are to start and finish every endeavor. Everything that is tried and tested in the life of a Christian should, without a doubt, first line up with the will of God.

To be equipped for battle is to have at least a basic knowledge and understanding of the spiritual realm as a tool for fighting the enemy. The importance of the various weapons of spiritual warfare is taken from the biblical texts and is explained in the study. Though these passages are well-known and very familiar they are too often misunderstood and misconstrued. The chapter on the Weapons of Warfare was designed to be beneficial to the Church in encouraging the practice of using the weapons with which He has equipped believers. These weapons are for the pastors, preachers, teachers, missionaries, evangelists, and all other ministers and believers of the Ministry of Jesus Christ.

If the mystery of Deliverance Ministry is revealed, the fear of ministering deliverance will also be diminished in the Body of Christ. This will present a domino effect in the Body of Christ and inevitably open the door for victory in the lives of believers. As victory becomes the dominant force in the lives of believers, the forces of darkness becomes dismantled and destroyed. Spiritual matters are very complex issues and in many instances can-

Taught vs Revealed

not be taught in the natural way, as some assume. Spiritual matters must be *revealed*. As the Church gains knowledge and understanding about the purpose and benefits of healing and deliverance in the Body of Christ, the revelation of the Word of God will come to the believers with a significant urgency of demonstration and power. The Word of God does not come without results.

Few ministries (lay or clerical) in the Christian Church have been as subject to misunderstanding as the "Ministry of Deliverance." Teachings about this ministry have led to confusion and concern on the part of Christian pastors and parishioners alike. What's worse, many Spirit-filled Christians knowledgeable of the Bible wrestle with the spiritual forces of darkness. My personal observation of this phenomenon led me to reexamine my own notion that evil forces were associated only with non–Christians' need for deliverance (salvation). I realized that I understood very little about the biblical truths declared through the Deliverance Ministry of Jesus. As I examined my preconceptions in light of biblical teachings on Deliverance Ministry, I began to see how God's salvation plan revealed throughout the Bible embraces and clarifies the ministry of deliverance.

In some quarters in the Church, believers worry that any discussion about the enemy (Satan) gives him glory. Deliverance ministry has, in too many quarters, been reduced to supernatural phenomena as in the genre of Christian fiction known as "spiritual warfare" novels, which feature hideous, evil, fictitious characters and ideas. We in the Body of Christ have too often resorted to vain clichés uttered without conviction or power. By the authority of Jesus Christ we will ultimately take back what the devil has stolen from us, but unfortunately we have lost much ground in authority, dominion, and power. This book will present a biblical worldview of Deliverance Ministry because God is restoring authentic, biblically-based deliverance ministry to the Body of Christ in a magnanimous way in these end times.

When we allow the biblical worldview to inform our worldview it will debunk the fear of spiritual forces of wickedness and give clarity to our dominion, authority, and power over the enemy. The scriptures proclaim that the blood of Jesus procures deliverance from spiritual bondage. The Church as the Body of Christ realizes Jesus' Deliverance Ministry when we boldly affirm that "believers have an enemy and need to be free from spiritual bondage." A proper understanding of the ministry of deliverance reveals that wherever a need exists there is a means of meeting that need. Jesus, the Great Deliverer, has the power to meet the need for deliverance. The spirit and the flesh will continuously battle until we are totally delivered by the Great Deliverer.

An accurate understanding of Deliverance Ministry is as vital in the present-day Church as it was in the earliest Church (as described in the Acts of the Apostles). The enemy has devised a plan to nullify the Deliverance Ministry, but God is a deliverer and deliverance is a hallmark of His plan. It is time for the Church to overcome the fear of Deliverance Ministry and realize that it is counterproductive to fear what we do not understand and then to attack what we fear. The reaction is natural, but the remedy is spiritual. When we take on the Spirit of God, we declare war against the enemy of God. The objectives of this book are: (1) to debunk myths about deliverance by recourse to the truth of the scriptures and thus suggest that we will have ultimate victory over sin (deliverance) through the wisdom of God, and (2) provide guidance to those who are called to serve in Deliverance Ministry.

This book is divided into two parts. Part 1 is the "theory" part that provides Deliverance Ministers with the necessary background knowledge and understanding of the history and context of Deliverance Ministry. Part 2 is the "practice" part that provides Deliverance Ministers with the skills and tools they need to diagnose and treat spiritual bondage.

PART I

Essential Knowledge for Deliverance Ministers

CHAPTER 1

What is Deliverance Ministry?

Origins of Christian Deliverance Ministry

The roots of Deliverance Ministry are in the earthly ministry of Jesus of Nazareth (as recorded in the Gospels of Matthew, Mark, Luke, and John). Everything Jesus did during His earthly ministry was performed as a man operating under the power of the Holy Spirit. He was the model of ministry for all who would follow Him in any office of Christian ministry. He was anointed by the Holy Spirit in His preaching, healing, and casting out demons. This includes Deliverance Ministry, which is a necessary Christian ministry because it is a viable means of advancing the gospel of Jesus Christ in its promotion of healing and restoration of the demonized (that is, those who are afflicted with evil spirits and under the enemy's influence). This is the "good news" (i.e., the gospel or *euangelos)* that declares even today that Jesus Christ is still in the business of healing and restoration. He is still setting the captives free.

Deliverance is Ministering Divine Grace

Deliverance Ministry is an expansive area of ministry that operates under the office of a person authorized in religious matters (e.g., a pastor, ordained minister, or evangelist). When operating at full capacity, the Deliverance Minister puts his or her ministry gifts to use as an expression of God's grace. Deliverance is a divine grace from Jesus for the wounded spirits, those who are bound, whose souls are bruised, whose hearts are demonized, and whose bodies are afflicted and diseased.

Deliverance Ministry is foremost a ministry that glorifies the Lord Jesus Christ by delivering captives (as in Jesus' initial proclamation of the mission of His ministry in Luke 4:19). When properly administered within the context of biblical teachings, deliverance brings freedom, clarity, and the reality of a life "in Christ." This sheds light on the concept of first being delivered from error to truth. Freedom from spiritual bondage brings God's people within direct contact of the kingdom of God. For as Jesus said in Luke 11:20, *"But if I with the finger of God cast out devils, no doubt the kingdom of God is come upon you."*

To be delivered is to *be rescued from a situation of grave danger*—a situation from which it is impossible for one to free himself or herself. *Deliverance is rescue by a greater power.* Even though all Christian believers are vested with the power and authority through Jesus Christ over the powers of darkness to cast out demons, it is the Word of God through the Holy Spirit that has the potential to set captive souls free. Deliverance does not operate independently of the Word of God. So in order for deliverance to become a permanent part of one's lifestyle, it is first necessary for the foundational hearing, understanding, and teaching of the Word of God to become a part of one's life. The truth of the Word of God is absolute, transparent, and void of any deceit. God's truth must be declared and sought after in the quest for authentic Christian living—for ordained clergy and the priesthood of all believers alike. Truth certainly cannot be held hostage by the devices Satan and his evil surrogates conjure up. The promised result of salvation is victory over spiritual and physical death and entering into eternal life with Him.

START WITH?

Deliverance Ministry Must Focus on the Root Cause of Bondage

Deliverance Ministry is sometimes hindered because the root causes of the bondage (from which one needs to be delivered) are not addressed. The scriptures make this clear in the teaching and preaching of the Gospel. For many believers, it is a sobering realization that the afflictions of their daily lives are the results of demonic assaults. These assaults can pertain to the body, mind, emotions, or will—areas of the soul that Satan desires to dominate, manipulate, and ultimately control. Tragically, many of the assaults on God's people are strategic and personal. No one on earth is exempt from a plan devised by a satanic thug to steal, kill, and destroy.

Deliverance is *"freedom."* The word "free" as expressed in these New Testament passages suggests that it is synonymous with deliverance:

- **Romans 8:2:** "For the law of the Spirit of life in Christ Jesus has made me free (delivered) from the law of sin and death."

- **Romans 6:18:** "Being then made free (delivered) from sin."

- **Romans 6:20:** "You were free (delivered) from righteousness."

- **Romans 7:3:** "Be dead, she is free (delivered) from that law."

- **Galatians 5:1:** "Wherewith Christ has made us free (delivered)."

- **Galatians 3:28:** "There is neither bond nor free (delivered)."

Thus, deliverance can be considered the process by which God intervenes and breaks the yoke of the enemy by means of human vessels. Please understand that, though human vessels are used to accomplish deliverance, the ultimate means of bringing about the results (i.e., deliverance) is the power of the Holy Spirit. The precise means of accomplishing deliverance are as diverse as the situations from which a person needs to be delivered. The presence of demonic spirits is typically revealed by the "discerning of spirits," which is one of the gifts of the Holy Spirit listed in 1 Corinthians 12:10. There is no room in the practice of Deliverance Ministry for human pride or self-proclaimed glory. Deliverance is indeed a work of God, and any display of egotistical self-importance on the part of the one called to serve as Deliverance Minister is a potential entry point for the enemy to frustrate the process. All of God's glory belongs to God.

A deliverance session can be as simple as a repenting confession or exhalation of a deep breath or as complex as many days and weeks of counseling, fasting, and praying for spiritual discernment to break strongholds, curses, witchcraft, and other types of diabolical activity. Deliverance requires hearing from God and being sensitive to the work of the Holy Spirit. A spiritual meaning of *deliverance* is acknowledging the grace of God in spite of one's condition. This is fundamental to the proper understanding of salvation.

The Perils of Denying Deliverance Ministry

One consequence of denying the ministry of deliverance is that it *seriously limits the effectiveness of the Church in fulfilling its mission.* Whenever blatant denial of the need for and practice of Delivery Ministry is present in the Church, evil forces are left to go

unchallenged and unchecked in the Body of Christ. It is imperative that believers become sensitive to the divine wisdom of God
and affirm that believers have a legal right to be free and the right
to set captives free. Jesus declared that He came to bestow abundant life on His followers, which implies not only that they will
be consecrated but also free from bondage. When members of
the Body of Christ are in torment and suffering, enslaved and in
bondage, they are living an impoverished life (the opposite of an
abundant life) and the consequences are far-reaching. The price
of being in bondage is higher than the price of being delivered.
Deliverance Ministry exists to provide them with deliverance and
freedom in Christ Jesus. There is a definite price to pay for both
bondage and freedom. Though humans have the capacity to
choose whether they will commit a particular sin, they cannot
choose whether they will be sinners or not. They can only acknowledge the fact that the past has affected the present, and the
present will ultimately affect the future.

Satan will continue working his plan to to deceive God's people through various diabolical methods, but the truth of the
Word extinguishes the deception of the enemy. Truth is uncom-
promising, unyielding, and never surrenders or bows to anything
less than truth. As such, truth is the only path to spiritual freedom and a necessary factor in true deliverance. Believers must be
willing to be delivered from error to truth. Even though they
know the truth, believers will at times resist it. Thus, merely
knowing the truth is not enough; for the devil knows the truth,
believes the truth, and trembles before God. James 2:19 says:

> *"Thou believest that there is one God; thou doest well:*
> *the devils also believe, and tremble."*

In order to comprehend truth, mankind must believe and receive the divine Word of God. As one expressed so well, "Truth is

spiritually revealed, the understanding of truth is intellectually determined."

● Deliverance is Not Just for Unbelievers

Deliverance is contingent on abiding in the work of Jesus on the cross, for it was He who made believers free. The Bible says believers have been delivered and set free from the powers of darkness, which Christ Jesus accomplished on the cross. Why, then, we might ask are Christians in the Body of Christ still in need of deliverance? The answer lies not in who believers are (in Christ) but where they are (in body). Christians are in need of deliverance because they are called to be *in the world* (to live *in* the world though they are not *of* the world), and the world at present (and this present age) is the domain of the evil one. In his prayer on behalf of His disciples, Jesus prayed (John 17:9-14):

> "I pray for them: I pray not for the world, but for them which thou hast given me; for they are thine. And all mine are thine and thine are mine; and I am glorified in them. And now I am no more in the world, but these are in the world, and I come to thee. Holy Father, keep through thine own name those whom thou hast given me, that they may be one as we are. While I was with them in the world, I kept them in thy name: those that thou gavest me I have kept and none of them is lost, but the son of perdition; that the scripture might be fulfilled. And now come I to thee; and these things I speak in the world that they might have my joy fulfilled in themselves. I have given them thy word; and the world hath hated them, but thou shouldest keep them from the evil. They are not of the world, even as I am not of the

world. Sanctify them through truth: thy word is truth."

Unless believers live in perfect holiness and devotion to God and the things of God, they will struggle in many areas and thus give an opening to the works of Satan. Thus, when a believer is in a situation that causes him to be in bondage, he is effectively rendered powerless to respond to the works of Satan. He has lost his spiritual authority. When believers are unable to subdue fleshly passions, they give place to the devil and bondage becomes a reality. Bondage is the loss of freedom, and loss of freedom indicates the need for deliverance. Bondage occurs when evil forces assume control of their actions and threaten their well-being.

The enemy strives to keep man in bondage through the use of these various methods, such as:

- **Legal bonds** (contract, covenant, commandment, decree, pledge, promise, mandate)

- **Emotional attachments** (affinities, kinship, likeness, alliances, interrelationships)

- **Physical bonds** (restraints, handcuffs, fetters, tie)

- **Psychological bonds** (mental enslavement, servitude, subjection, yoke)

These are the same tactics and devices used in the old, unregenerate mindset before man's mind is regenerated in salvation. These tactics are part of the enemy's diabolical schemes to tempt the natural man. This underscores the importance of a regenerated mind. The natural man can be influenced by either the "Holy Spirit" or the "spirit of the world." The Holy Spirit expresses itself through the body of man by the "regenerated spirit of man." Evil spirits express their evil deeds through the body of

Believe in propriation to
Sanctification
aerin

man by the soul of man. "Evil spirits" are spiritual beings that are enemies of God and man. They rely on man's traditional way of thinking to accomplish their objectives in mankind. The Bible says, however, that believers have received a renewed mind in Christ and the Spirit of God.

unbeliever
-deliverition
salvation

> "Now we have received, not the spirit of the world,
> but the Spirit which is of God; that we might know
> the things that are freely given to us of God"
> —1 Corinthians 2:12

It is vital that all believers realize they are subject to the things that pertain to the spiritual realm. These include the Holy Spirit, angels (or messengers) of God, as well as the influence of evil spirits. The conflict in the spiritual realm is what we call "spiritual warfare." Spiritual warfare is the process by which deliverance is accomplished. Dr. Ed Murphy (1996), in *The Handbook for Spiritual Warfare*, stated:

> "Spiritual warfare is revealed as a part of God's War-
> rior Kingdom in ongoing conflict with internal evil
> (the flesh), social evil (the world), and supernatural
> evil (the spirit world)."

He further described spiritual warfare as a multi-dimensional sin war. The Church is at war with evil and, with the authority and power believers have in Christ, believers are to challenge the principalities and powers that hold God's people in bondage. Spiritual warfare touches every dimension of human life. The belief that the battle is over once one accepts the plan of salvation is not biblically sound. The Word of God says that Jesus was confronted with demons as He walked the earth in bodily form. Therefore, if we be in Christ, like Him, we will experience the attacks of the enemy as well.

In the deliverance process, a victim or captive of the devil is led out of bondage or unhealthy demonic dependencies into spiritual freedom. This is done by faith and in the authority of Christ Jesus. Jesus gave believers authority and power over the powers of the enemy. Authority is the *right* to *rule;* power is the *ability* to rule. If a man is not delivered from the issues of his sinful flesh, he will not overcome the flesh. Rather, he will be overcome by the law of the flesh, and the flesh will dominate in his life. This type of person is considered a *carnal* Christian in the Body of Christ.

In Romans 7:21-25, Paul wrote:

> *"I find then a law, that when I would do good, evil is present with me. For I delight in the law of God after the inward man; But I see another law in my members, warring against the law of my mind, and bringing me into captivity to the law of sin which is in my members. O wretched man that I am! Who shall deliver me from the body of this death? I thank God through Jesus Christ our Lord. So then with the mind I myself serve the law of God; but with the flesh the law of sin."*

• Deliverance Ministry: A Challenging Call

Deliverance Ministry is a very challenging ministry—one that requires patience, compassion, time, and prayer. It is so challenging, in fact, that not many are willing to become involved in ministering deliverance. What's more, there is no glory in Deliverance Ministry, for the glory belongs to the Lord. Every minister of deliverance must be humble and meek while boldly exercising the authority and power of Christ over the evil one and his surrogates. The key to the actual process of deliverance is the exercise of spiritual authority.

The satisfaction in deliverance results from seeing believers healed and set free by the power of God. Seeing firsthand the people of God being snatched from the torment and pain of demonic influence and set free into a life of peace and joy in the Holy Ghost is a phenomenal experience. Many people are lost in darkness and misery, and many die without help in varying states of oppression, obsession, suppression, and depression. A deliverance ministry helps such tormented souls by enlisting their cooperation in the process of deliverance (i.e., by exercising faith and authority bestowed by Jesus on all believers).

The Ministry of Deliverance requires that the minister lead a life that reflects purity and holiness. The danger here, which must be considered and taken very seriously, is that the Deliverance Minister will bring harm to himself as well as the person to whom she or he is ministering. Demonic forces are diabolic angels of a higher intelligence and in many instances they will attack the one seeking to thwart their mission (robbing, killing, and destroying the lives of God's people). The Bible, however, admonishes believers to "fear not." God is faithful and equips His people to be vessels of honor, and a vessel of honor for Jesus has always been, and always will be, a threat to the kingdom of darkness.

CHAPTER 2

What is God's Deliverance Plan?

GOD'S DELIVERANCE PLAN as revealed in the Bible ever since the "fall" of mankind served to show all humanity the need for a Savior to restore and save man from the fatal consequences of the fall. Through Moses, God gave His people moral laws to govern their behavior and show man that there was a penalty for sin. Atonement for sin under the Mosaic law consisted of sacrificing animals as payment for breaking the law. Throughout the Old Testament, however, man proved unable to keep the law of God. From the blessings of Abraham to the urging of the Prophets, the people consistently failed, even in the midst of promises of blessing. God showed man that he has no ability to live independent of God, nor can he become reunited with God without the help of God Himself.

Thus, God did a new thing. By grace, God became man in the form of Jesus, the first to be born both physically and spiritually alive. Jesus came as an example to demonstrate to believers how it was possible for a spiritually-alive person could live a righteous life, even in the midst of the enemy's temptations.

God's Deliverance Plan, according *to Foundations of Pentecostal Theology*, states:

> "Having dealt with the doctrine of Theology, wherein the Holiness of God was emphasized, and having seen the failure and sin of Mankind in the study of Anthropology and Hamartiology,

one is brought to realize the utter need for a plan of salvation sufficient to bridge the vast gap between these two infinite extremes" (*Man's Sinfulness and God's Holiness, p. 179*).

Types & Prophecies

The truth is that God provided a way to bridge the gap between these two infinite extremes to redeem the human race back to Him. Deliverance and salvation are based entirely on the work of Christ as mediator between sinful man, on the one hand, and a holy offended God, on the other. This truth is revealed in the books of the Old Testament through the following types and prophecies (Ingram, 2006):

Types:

- **The Coats of Skins** *(Genesis 3:21)*
  "Unto Adam also and to his wife did the Lord God make coats of skins, and clothed them."

- **Abel's Offering** *(Genesis 4:4)*
  "And Abel, he also brought of the firstlings of his flock and of the fat thereof. And the Lord has respect unto Abel and to his offering."

- **The offering of Isaac** *(Genesis 22:2)*
  "And he said, take now thy son, thine only son Isaac, whom thou lovest, and get thee into the land of Moriah; and offer him there for a burnt offering upon one of the mountains which I will thee of."

- **The Passover Lamb** *(Exodus 12:13)*
  "And the blood shall be to you for a token upon the houses

*where ye are; and when I see the plague shall not be upon you
to destroy you, when I smite the land of Egypt."*

Prophecy:

- **The Seed of the Woman** *(Genesis 3:15) "The First Gospel."*
  *"And I will put enmity between thee and the woman, and
  between thy seed and her seed; it shall bruise thy head, and
  thou shalt bruise his heel" (Protevangelium).*

The New Testament Gospels reveal that Jesus' sacrifice satisfied God's righteous demands; the only basis on which a holy
God could forgive sin was by His own sinless Son's bearing the
penalty of sin. In God's deliverance plan, grace is not merely
something that God expresses but an expression of what He is.
Arthur W. Pink wrote:

> "Grace is a provision for men who are so fallen
> that they cannot help themselves, so corrupt that
> they cannot change their natures, so averse to
> God that they cannot turn to Him, so blind they
> cannot see Him, so deaf they cannot hear Him, so
> dead that He Himself must open their graves and
> lift them into resurrection. Grace is the means by
> which we are saved, however we are kept by the
> power of God through faith, which is a gift of
> God. Throughout the scripture we see the revela-
> tion of God's deliverance plan as His people are
> justified by faith, regenerated by the Holy Spirit,
> sanctified in Christ, and finally glorified at His re-
> turn according to (Romans 8:32-34)."

Deliverance and Salvation

Deliverance and salvation are the terms used to describe the active and complex process involved in delivering the human soul unto salvation. It is the rescue, recovery, and restoration work of God's redemptive purpose in retrieving us from sin and death. Deliverance is the term used to explain God's most powerful work of divine grace in our lives. Deliverance and salvation are a proactive part of God's total redemptive plan, as the power of the Holy Spirit is actively setting-free, rescuing, liberating, and working out the plan of God for His people.

It is within God's plan for man to encounter spiritual warfare; the true spiritual conflict, however, is between God and Satan, good and evil, flesh and spirit. Spiritual warfare is a salvation issue for the unbeliever, *not* for the believer. The unbeliever's spiritual warfare is in receiving Christ as Lord and Savior. When one chooses to live spiritually in Christ, this is a direct attack on the enemy's kingdom. At the very point of receiving Christ, the enemy will always make a final attempt to stop the unbeliever. Whenever the unbeliever is in a position to hear the Word of God, spiritual warfare is inevitable. The unbeliever will surely become engaged in warfare, whether he realizes it or not. The enemy never wants the unbeliever to adhere to the Word of God.

Hebrews 4:12 states:

> *"For the Word of God is quick, and powerful, and sharper than any two edged sword, piercing even to the dividing asunder of soul and spirit, and of the joints and marrow, and is a discerner of the thoughts and intents of the heart."*

On the other hand, those who have been saved—those who are in the Body of Christ—face sanctification issues with being in the state of sanctification: holy, pure, consecrated, and separated in the sense of being morally and spiritually cleansed. Believers face problems with the fact that God calls for a holy people separated from sin and every profane and defiling thing and living a life consecrated to Him. Separation from sin and being set apart for a sacred purpose is a grace given to us by God: We are blessed with the grace to be holy. In Romans 12:1-2, Paul states:

> *"I beseech you therefore, brethren, by the mercies of God, that ye present your bodies a living sacrifice, holy, acceptable unto God, which is your reasonable service. And be not conformed to this world; but be ye transformed by the renewing of your mind, that ye may prove what is that good, and acceptable, and perfect, will of God."*

Therefore, the grace of God has made provision in the redemptive plan for sanctification and regeneration through the work of the Holy Spirit. This work was done at the new birth, by the indwelling of the Holy Spirit, as well as through the ongoing intercessory ministry of Jesus on behalf of believers. In 1 Corinthians 10:13, Paul states:

> *"There hath no temptation taken you but such as is common to man: but God is faithful, who will not suffer you to be tempted above that ye are able; but will with the temptation also make a way to escape, that ye may be able to bear it."*

In the New Testament the meaning for the word salvation is based on the Greek word *soteria,* the meanings of which include preservation from:

- enemies

- molestation and bondage

- spiritual and natural forces

In Romans 5:12, Paul states:

"Wherefore, as by one man sin entered into the world, and death by sin; and so death passed upon all men, for that all have sinned;

Death entered the world through the fall of man. Death always comes through sin and is the perpetual result of sin. Death has penetrated the soul, spirit, and body of all men. There is no part of man that has not been marred by the taint of sin. This is the reason man has to receive the life of Jesus Christ. The way of salvation cannot come as a result of man's own desire to make amends, for death is irreversible. Sin had to be judged before there can be deliverance or rescue from eternal death. This has been provided by the Deliverance Plan of God or the Salvific Plan of God.

The branch of theology that deals with salvation is called Soteriology. Soteriology encompasses the total work of God in bringing men from the state of sin to the state of glory through Jesus Christ. Simply put: Salvation brings man from spiritual death to eternal life. The single condition for salvation is faith. Faith is both the gift of God and the responsibility of man.

Salvation Begins with Confession

Salvation is not a single act of confessing "Jesus is Lord" with one's mouth, yet the Christian life does indeed begin with a "confession of faith," a public declaration before witnesses that says Jesus is Lord and declares that one belongs to Him. Salvation accomplishes many things, such as:

- **Redemption**–means full release based on payment of a ransom price (2 Peter 2:1).

- **Reconciliation**–means that because of Christ's death, man's relationship with God has been changed from a state of enmity to one of fellowship (Romans 5:10).

- **Propitiation**–means that God's wrath has been turned away by the offering of Christ (Romans 3:25).

Why is the confession of faith a condition for salvation? First, the mouth gives outward expression of the thoughts of the mind. A spoken word is the external manifestation of a person's character. This means the mouth is the organ through which our relationship with God is made sure. Words are thoughts of the heart, and the heart the mind of man.

The Bible says, *"As a man thinks in his heart, so is he."* In other words, *we are what we think.* Confession is continuously made until the final deliverance is made (salvation) from natural life unto eternal life. Confession gives the Holy Spirit the legal right to take residence (indwelling) and authority in one's spirit and to inaugurate a lifelong progressive work on the inside.

In Romans 10:9–10, Paul states:

> *"That if thou shalt confess with thy mouth the Lord Jesus, and shalt believe in thine heart that God hath raised him from the dead, thou shalt be saved. For with the heart man believeth unto righteousness, And with the mouth confession is made unto salvation."*

Transformation: Having the Mind of Christ

Confession is the catalyst that starts regeneration, the process by which we who are spiritually dead (Ephesians 2:1) are made alive to God and are "born again." Because regeneration is a work of God within us by which He gives us new life, it is considered an instantaneous event. Yet it only happens once, and the believer does not know exactly when this change occurs. We do know, however, that once we change our mind, we change our life.

Acquiring a "renewed mind" is a process of transformation and the key to receiving spiritual freedom. When the mind is renewed, we have the *"mind of Christ"* (Philippians 2:5-8). Since the mind is renewed through our connection with the Holy Spirit, the renewed mind is operating on a higher level, Satan no longer has control over the believer. Thus, believers are in the world but not conformed to the world (not *of* the world). Believers can live in the world without being governed by the standards of the world, and they can maintain control over their minds. This is walking in spiritual freedom versus spiritual bondage. Isaiah 26:3 tells us that *"He will keep him in perfect peace whose mind is stayed on Him."*

Because the words *heart* and *mind* used in the Bible refer to man's spiritual nature, the heart is symbolic of the mind in many instances. Thus, precise definitions of the term "heart" are difficult. The meaning of *heart* as used in Dr. Ed Murphy's *Handbook for Spiritual Warfare* is:

> "The heart as the core of man, the inner man, the spirit-man; that central agency and facility within man whereby he imagines, intends, purposes and thinks and understands."

The heart is also that essence and inner substance of man that constitutes the core and seat of emotions, the center of emotional reaction, feeling, and sensitivity. The heart then holds the issues and motives of spiritual life. It is the part of man that God searches and will be reconciled and redeemed back to God.

> *"Keep thy heart (delivered) with all diligence; for*
> *out of it are the issues of life." (Proverbs 4:23)*

The mind is the seat of thought, passions, desires, appetites, and intents of the heart. It is the place within whereby man imagines, thinks, understands, and remembers. The mind is therefore one's life, soul, appetite, person, and finally it is what makes a person who he is: the total person (oneself). Jesus instructed us:

> *"And you shall love the Lord your God with all your*
> *heart, with all your soul, with all your mind, and*
> *with all your strength." (Mark 12:30)*

Deliverance from the Lusts of the Flesh

Man's salvation is secured by the grace of God and the blood of the cross. The acts of being delivered and ministering deliverance express God's desire for believers to live a victorious and prosperous life, void of spiritual and physical bondage and consisting of spiritual and physical freedom. The Body of Christ will never experience how wonderful it is to serve the Lord without heavy burdens and hindrances until believers deal with the flesh. The flesh is the carnal, evil part of man that harbors the enemy and is in rebellion against God. It is the evil within mankind that gives him the propensity to engage in every evil work—internal and external. The flesh has been referred to as the *fountainhead of all sins*.

The flesh is arrogant and prideful and will maintain a self-righteous attempt to distort the Word of God. The flesh has no conscience; it has been sentenced to death and cannot be saved, redeemed, or rescued. It paralyzes the spiritually-sound life of the believer and is in opposition to the Word of God. This is why it is mandatory that anyone engaging in the ministry of deliverance have and maintain a high level of spiritual maturity. Demons have no place and no right to live inside people who are spiritually clean. To be spiritually clean is to be holy, dedicated and devoted to God, and separated from sin. Holiness speaks of wholeness with all parts well, healthy, and in operation.

Man's capacity to sin, however, is without question. For as Paul stated: *"All have sinned and fall short of the glory of God"* *(Romans 3:23)*. God's plan is that man would live in total harmony and fellowship with Him. As soon as man sinned, God immediately executed His plan of escape. God's plan for man is not predicated on what man does but rather on *who God is*. God's plan has never changed; from the foundations of the world God knew the plan. To change His plan would mean changing who He is, putting His reputation, His name, His word would be on the line. God's Word says, *"For I am the Lord, I change not"* (Malachi 3:6). God is still working out His plan of deliverance and salvation.

In His wisdom and under His own counsel, God sent His Son to earth to live and die in human form, "fully man" as the apostolic creeds expressed it, but without sin. Following the fall of Adam and Eve, God pronounced his curse, part of which states:

> *"And I will put enmity between thee and the woman, and between thy seed and her seed; it shall bruise thy head, and thou shalt bruise his heel" (Genesis 3:15).*

In this text we see that a prophecy was pronounced: The offspring of woman would crush the head of the serpent. Jesus was the prophesied "offspring of the woman" (having been born of Mary without agency of a human father). Jesus has indeed crushed the serpent's (Satan's) head. No one could take Jesus' life. He chose to lay down His life and faced death voluntarily. Jesus was the sacrifice for the whole world. The way was made for God's people to enter eternal life in heaven (thus escaping the wages of sin—death). The rescue plan was completed on the cross; the sinless blood of Jesus has redeemed mankind and satisfied the debt. We are free "in Christ Jesus" indeed.

Paul wrote in Romans 8:1: *"There is therefore now no condemnation to those who are in Christ Jesus.* It is through the Word of God that the Spirit of Christ releases all believers from bondage. Jesus is the One who brings the gospel of salvation, deliverance, healing, and restoration to those in bondage. Many times in the ministry of healing and deliverance the desire is for God to deal with the symptoms rather than the cause. The person wants relief from the torment and suffering experienced in his life but is reluctant to make Jesus Lord of his life. Paul says in Romans 8:21 that he looks for the whole creation to be free from bondage and decay. True deliverance does not merely treat the symptom but cures the cause of the bondage.

Healing & Deliverance: Necessary Elements of Christian Ministry

Healing and deliverance are necessary components in the ministry of Jesus. They are included in the Great Commission that Jesus gave to the Church. God's deliverance plan was detailed and absolute. Mankind does *nothing* to merit salvation. There are no restrictions on the gospel, and it is free to all; it needs only to be accepted. It is a gospel (good news) for the poor as well as for the rich. It is through the teaching and preaching of the gospel that believers are set free from demonic influences and are able to remain free from the sin and struggles that have bound them.

Again, the Bible says it is a free gift of God, and yet the price is still too steep for some, for it does indeed cost everything pertaining to you.

The Blood and Salvation

The theme of the gospel is the death and resurrection of Jesus and the salvation and redemption available to all through the shed blood of Jesus. Deliverance is God's plan, and God alone set the standard and established the exchange. The blood of the Lamb was the only suitable exchange for such hideous transgressions in a world polluted with sin and death. Our common bond and fellowship with God is emphatically the blood of Jesus. The writer of Hebrews (Hebrews 10:10-14) expressed it this way:

> *"By which will we are sanctified through the offering of the body of Jesus Christ once for all. And every priest standeth daily ministering and offering oftentimes the same sacrifices, which can never take away sins: But this man, after he had offered one sacrifice for sins for ever, sat down on the right hand of God; From henceforth expecting till his enemies be made his footstool. For by one offering he hath perfected for ever them that are sanctified."*

God has made peace with His creation through the blood of Jesus. Jesus' blood transferred and released the power and communicable attributes of the Godhead onto mankind through the Holy Spirit. The blood of Jesus is the earnest assurance of a perfect salvation. It has irresistible power to destroy sin and opens the way to heaven for all who accept God's free gift of grace by faith. Jesus was raised from the grave through the blood. Blood is the essence of all life, and life in its entirety is God's mystery. The blood by its power is able to sustain believers in their daily walk with Christ. Deliverance is by means of the blood that protects, cleanses, and justifies.

Deliverance is a result of the blood. No human factor played any part in the deliverance of humanity from the bondage of sin and death; it is of the divine wisdom and counsel of God. Deliverance by the blood was a requirement of God before the foundations of the world. Blood holds the essence of life, which is the mystery of God, yet blood is the exchange for sin and death. The blood of Jesus was the blood of innocence because no acts of sin had contaminated it, for Jesus did not inherit Adam's sin nature—transmitted in the blood of man. This aspect gave a higher caliber of blood making it a most excellent sacrifice.

Hebrews 10:19-22 states:

> *"Therefore, brothers, since we have confidence to enter the Most Holy Place by the blood of Jesus, by a new and living way opened for us through the curtain, that is, his body, and since we have a great priest over the house of God, let us draw near to God with a sincere heart in full assurance of faith, having our hearts sprinkled to cleanse us from a guilty conscience and having our bodies washed with pure water."*

The death of Jesus is the essence of Christianity that sets it apart from all other religions. Christ crucified is the core preaching (proclamation) of the gospel. Because Jesus was crucified and died for the sins of humanity, believers have peace with God and the blood qualifies them as partakers of Jesus' inheritance. Through the blood of redemption, believers experience total eradication of sin expressed in:

- **Forgiveness**—the removal of all accusations from the sinner, pardon, involving restoration of broken relationships;

no longer feeling resentment for wrongs and offenses. Release from judgments and freedom from penalty. Only God can forgive sin.

- **Reconciliation**—the act of uniting man to God. The blood was shed to unite humans with God; having accomplished its work it will be perfected in us, including the removal of the offense that caused the disruption of peace and harmony.

- **Expiation**—atonement, purification, and the total removal of sin: *"Behold the Lamb of God that takes away the sin of the world."* By the shedding of His blood He bore full punishment for sin.

- **Justification**—being made righteous by an act of God (the righteousness of Jesus); by the blood believers have been fully justified and thus have a legitimate righteous claim to a place in heaven in the presence of a holy God.

- **Ransom**—the price paid by Christ to satisfy God's requirements. The blood testifies that it has cleansed the believer, who can meet death with the assurance that the power of the blood opens the door and makes us fit for heaven.

- **Propitiation**—appeasing and satisfying God's righteousness through the death of Jesus. The Blood of the Lamb gives the believers a right to heaven.

- **Substitution**—the dying of Jesus on behalf of the sinner (Isaiah 53:5).

- **Sanctification**—being set apart to be used by God, to be cleansed and separated from sin; the blood sanctifies be-

lievers for the emptying of ourselves that God may fill us
with Himself.

- **Atonement**—all that was accomplished by the death of
Christ (the total redemption of man).

The purchase or redemption (buy-back) of man through the
blood of Jesus renders the transaction not merely physical (i.e.,
the condition of the blood reveals the health or sickness of the
flesh) because, aside from the blood's being the essence of physical life, blood is the currency of all life. On Calvary's Cross, it was
the blood of Jesus that enabled all mankind to receive the remis-
sion of sin and eternal life. To accept the blood of Jesus is to
live—to live eternally in right relationship with God—and to reject the blood is to die and be eternally separated from God. This
intricate detail makes the Bible distinct from all other books because it contains a Word (Jesus) that is alive because of the power
of the blood of the Lord and Savior Jesus Christ.

Leviticus 17:11 declares that "life" is in the blood of the flesh:

> *"For the life of the flesh (of Jesus) is in the blood (of Je-*
> *sus), and I have given it to you upon the altar to*
> *make an atonement for your souls for it is the blood*
> *that maketh an atonement for the soul."*

The blood of Jesus transcends time and space, and, in the
realm of the spirit, it has an establishing voice as well as divine intelligence. The blood of Jesus speaks to God on behalf of believers bearing witness to our atonement without ceasing. Hebrews
10:22 states:

> *"Let us draw near with a true heart in full assurance*
> *of faith, having our hearts sprinkled from an evil con-*
> *science, and our bodies washed with pure waters."*

Believers' heart and conscience are cleansed by the blood of Jesus, and so also is their understanding and will, thoughts and desires. By the power of Christ's death and resurrection, sinful lusts and tendencies are extinguished. The blood of Jesus ensure that believers are free from all sins in what it called the "once for all" means of redemption. Hebrews 9:26 (Amplified) states:

> "For then would He often have had to suffer [over and over again] since the foundation of the world. But as it now is, He has once for all at the consummation and close of the ages appeared to put away and abolish sin by His sacrifice [of Himself]. We are delivered by the blood immediately through substitution from the judgment of God."

The Christian's deliverance is planned by God Himself. It is God's judgment that we must be rescued from sin and its consequence—death. It is God alone who can make a way of escape. Deliverance by the blood of the Lamb was by divine wisdom. If man desires to be delivered, he must be submissive to God and totally dependent on Him. It has been said that in this life one thing is certain—death. And death comes unexpectedly and with it, judgment. God's judgment, however, will come with power and will not be extinguished through all eternity.

CHAPTER 3

Deliverance & the Love of God

The Importance of Agape Love

One definition of *agape* love is *"God defined."* The Apostle John stated very clearly that "God is Love" (1 John 4:8). This is a biblical truth declared throughout the universe, and it is able to stand on its own grounds. Human love is a natural emotion that flows toward the object of one's affections. The natural man is of the flesh, and his life and perspective on love is consequently of the flesh and thus weak and imperfect at best.

The American Heritage Dictionary defines love as "an intense affection for another person based on familiar or personal ties." The dictionary definition of love implies that love is based on a desire for self-fulfillment of a condition that we personally require. On the contrary, the love of God is that standard or quality of love that continues even when the person fails to live up to His expectations. This concept of "agape love"—love without conditions or self-interests (with a pure motive) is the foundational principle of God's relationship with all of His creation. This is especially true with the objects of His love—humans—whom He created in His image. Not only is God love, but God is "in love" with humans. This is His one and only motive for delivering and saving sinful human beings.

One of the greatest gifts God has given to mankind is the gift of "God Himself" (God is Love). This perfect and most precious gift was given without our permission, consent, approval, or ap-plause. In a world fraught with suffering, sickness, and despair, Jesus' love is manifested in His compassion, healing, and deliver-ance of the downtrodden and captive. In most instances, this gift of God Himself goes without ever being acknowledged. It is not merely the gift of being alive, though the gift of life is from God and is the mystery of God. The absolutely perfect gift of God is God. This is expressed in John 3:16, which reveals the ultimate expression of "agape love." Love begets love; the only sufficient source of true love is a sovereign, loving God Himself.

The Bible: Chronicle of God's Love & Deliverance

From Genesis 1 onward, we see the love of God. God's love is a natural expression of all that He created and thus the expression was: *It is good*. As originally created the world—before sin en-tered the world and brought corruption— was good. What is God's goodness? Goodness in the sight of God is perfect, with-out error, flawless, and full of His splendor and glory. This was in everything God created because His creativity was born of His agape love. In his original state, having been made in the image of God, humankind had the ability here on earth to create out of love and the end result would be good. However, because we have another law in our being (Romans 7), even our creativity is contaminated and now subject to good and evil (i.e., from partak-ing of the fruit of the tree of the knowledge of good and evil in-stead of eating only from the tree of life).

Humans are created in God's image. God uses mankind to remind mankind that He is close to us. God chose to love man. This is an act of grace out of His own will. There is nothing we can do to make God love us. The mere fact that God is God, and God is love, means that it is His will to love us. God's love for us is absolute and cannot increase nor decrease because there is no change in God and thus no change in His love.

The biblical word *agape* was coined by the biblical authors from the verb *"agapao" (to love in a social or moral sense)*. This was to avoid the sensual associations of the Greek noun *"eros,"* which denoted sensual, sexual love.

The prevailing meaning of agape is the fact that agape love seeks to "give" rather than to receive. Giving is a consequence (a natural outflow) of love. People can religiously give without loving, but they cannot truly love without giving. This is true in both the natural and the spiritual realm.

This truth is reflected in every aspect of agape love. God is the greatest of all givers from the beginning of time. The scripture shows God's perfect love expressed through His continuous giving to His creation—giving life and light to a dark and void world, giving provisions for life, giving love to a people without reciprocation, giving a plan of salvation to those who are lost, and giving His Son to a world of sinners. *This* is agape love. The Psalmist asked, *"What is man that thou art mindful of him?" (Psalms 8:4).*

Agape love is the type of love that desires to satisfy the needs of the one who is loved rather than the needs of the lover. In fact, the one loved may be totally oblivious to the need of the one who is loving with agape. Despite the fact that God has no need and is self-sustained, void of all deficiency and lack, He is nevertheless attentive to and concerned with mankind's lack and needs. Perhaps the closest mankind ever comes to achieving the agape love of God is in the love of a mother for her child. In the Bible God states that His thoughts are not our thoughts and His ways are not our ways. The truth is, God's love is also not our love. God's loves satisfies our needs; we are the insatiable needy. Many times humans tend to reduce the love of God to the manner of love that we are accustomed to or familiar with. Humans naturally give love in the manner in which they desire to be loved to meet their own selfish needs and desires. This is sensual, self-gratifying love. It is not necessarily wrong, but it is not agape love at all.

Agape love is a love that satisfies the needs without necessarily satisfying the desires, the appetite, the flesh, or the carnal nature of man. Agape love is a love without limits, without reservations, and totally void of self-interest. Agape love never fails; there is no failure in God or His love.

From Genesis to Revelation, the creator is revealed as the only one qualified to assess the needs of His creation. The deliverance and salvation of man begins in Genesis 1, in the beginning, with the need of the first human to be rescued. Man was in a dilemma in the Garden; warfare was introduced to our family history. It was warfare in paradise. The love of God was there.

So agape was the word the New Testament writers used to capture the unconditional love of God. The two other words used in ordinary Greek for "love"—*philia* (dutiful or filial affection, brotherly love) and *eros* (passion, emotion, sensual love)—were not adequate to express the Christian concept of love. Agape love is unique because it is inclusive of God himself. It expresses the very nature of God. God does not love by reason or human logic. This exceptional standard of love is established by "the God who is Love."

Let us examine what the Bible says about love in some key passages.

- "He that loveth not knoweth not God; for **God is love**" (1 John 4:8). God's love is not established on any condition or specific quality in a person or thing being loved. God's love extends to and beyond all of His creation.

- "But God, who is rich in mercy for **His great love** wherewith he loved us" (Ephesians 2:4). Agape love with its exceptional qualities cares nothing about looks or acts, but is founded on a genuine concern for all people, even the unlovable, the vile, and offensive.

- "The Lord hath appeared of old unto me, saying. Yea, I have loved thee with an **everlasting love**; therefore with loving-kindness have I drawn thee" (Jeremiah 31:3).

- "May be able to comprehend with all saints what is the breadth, and length, and depth, and height; And to know the **love of Christ, which passeth knowledge,** that ye might be filled with all the fulness of God" (Ephesians 3:18-19).

- "Who shall separate us from the love of Christ? Shall tribulation, or distress, or persecution, or famine, or nakedness, or peril, or sword?" (Romans 8:35)

These passages of scripture confirm that "agape love" is the central theme of the entire Bible and is the climax of the New Testament. One of the greatest expressions of agape love in the New Testament is expressed in John 3:16:

> *"For God so loved the world, that he gave his only begotten Son, that whosoever believeth in him should not perish, but have everlasting life."*

This love is not for "the elect" only, but for the whole world. 1 Corinthinans 13 gives expression to agape love and its foundational importance. 1 Corinthians 13:1-5 declares:

> "If I speak in the tongues of men and of angels, but have not love, I am only a resounding gong or clanging cymbal. If I have the gift of prophecy and can fathom all mysteries and all knowledge, and if I have a faith that can move mountains, but have not love I am nothing. Even if I give all I possess to the poor and surrender my body to the flames, but have not love, I gain nothing. Love is patient, love is kind. It does not envy, it does not boast, it is not proud. It is not rude, it is not self-seeking, it is not easily angered, it keeps no record of wrongs."

Agape love is manifested in God's unconditional love and should be the way believers love each other and God. This love is most important because all else will pass away. Only love is eternal; it resides with God; it is the foundation of eternal life. When Jesus was asked by his disciples what the greatest commandment was, He said:

> "You shall love the Lord your God with all your heart, and with all your soul, and with all your mind" (Matthew 22:37).

This Agape love is a precious gift given to man before the foundations of the world. It does not function like the love of man. It is a love that is not intimidated by our insecurities, not scared of our situations, does not coy to our chaos, does not fear our foes, and does not magnifying our mistakes. What it does is hide our heart, cover our heads, search our souls, touch our temples (bodies), surround our territories, speak into our spirits, show our enemies, rock our boats and develop in us hope. Grace and mercy gives expression to the love of God throughout the Bible.

God's Love Revealed to Humankind

Humans were created in the image of God. This is one of the most powerful statements of truth in the Word of God. This statement of truth is what has Satan at such enmity with God and man. This truth means that man is absolutely on the mind of God. The word *image* is the root word for imagination, and in a broad sense the imagination of God holds the picture of man. God has no physical form. He is a spirit, and man is made in the image of God. And God is love. Thus humans are a picture of God's love. This is the epitome of God's love revealed to mankind. All of creation was made to show man how great God is, and how through this great love God has given to mankind authority, dominion, and power over all the creations on earth.

It is God's desire that humans—the "crown of His creation—know Him intimately as a God who is approachable and as a God of love. We love God because He first loved us. God has commanded us to love Him and our fellow human beings (our "neighbors"); this is the sum of all God's laws. If a man does not have the love of God in his heart, it is certain he has never been regenerated. God's love should motivate believers to keep His commandments because they love Him. The redemption of mankind makes it possible to love mankind through the agape love of God. 1 John 4:9-11 states:

> *"By this the love of God was manifested in us, that God has sent His only begotten Son into the world so that we might live through Him. In this is love, not that we loved God, but that He loved us and sent His*

Son to be the propitiation for our sins. Beloved, if
God so loved us, we also ought to love one another."

God's love is unconditional—not contingent on the worth,
performance, or responsiveness of the other. God manifests His
agape love towards mankind because human beings are born
spiritually separated from Him. Agape love is devoid of arrogance and results from the power of the filling ministry of the
Holy Spirit. Just as God love humans with agape love, so humans are called to and enabled in Christ to love each other and
God with agape love. As such, it is not love based on feelings of affection or romance toward God or another human. Unconditional love for God and neighbor is a loving response to God's unconditional love for humans. God's command that humans love
Him and their neighbor is indeed a law, for 1 John 5:3 states that
if we truly love God we will not only love all of His children but
will also keep His commandments and obey His teachings.
Agape love is always *expressed* and *active*. The work of the Holy
Spirit is to impart love.

God's agape love towards humans enables them to resist the
impulse to challenge and cause division, but encourages unity
and love and declares to the world that Christians are disciples of
Jesus Christ. Simply put, humankind is the result of God's love
and was conceived out of agape love. Humans are the children of
agape love born of an immaculate conception: *immaculate* meaning pure, clean, decent, perfect, above reproach and *conception*
meaning beginning, birth, origin, launching.

No Salvation Apart From Agape

Without agape love there could be no salvation. There is no condition in humanity after the fall that would merit God's love.
God's love for humankind is unconditional and independent of

humankind's worth, performance, or responsiveness. The love of God for humankind did rent the veil in the temple and carried the shame of Adam and Eve and covered their nakedness after they had consorted with another lover. Love united the true bride (Church) with the true groom (Jesus) and has broken the bond that covered our understanding. Agape love made it possible to penetrate the veil (flesh) and enter into the deep places of our soul and be intimate with God.

For humans, agape love is a result of the power of the filling ministry of the Holy Spirit and, as such, it is patient, unselfish, kind, believing, truthful, enduring, trusting, and hopeful. It is not boastful, jealous, rude, arrogant, selfish, or angry. It is pure and never fails. It appreciates the full meaning of Christ on the cross as agape love incarnate. To see Christ in the Gospels is to see agape love expressed in the human life of Christ. Love involves whatever services the situation demands. Jesus' love heals, teaches, defends, forgives, and comforts. The is the example He set for believers. This is the standard. Jesus' life on earth is always calling us to a higher standard where love governs the way we interact and care for each other.

Agape love enables us to see the answer and share our understanding with whomever is seeing or experiencing a problem. It is never judgmental; it is totally without expectations, demands, or requirements and is not subject to change, no matter what appears to change around it. It is unconditional forgiveness because it transcends the concept of needing forgiveness; it knows that humans are of a fleshly nature and thus does not hold misdeeds or bad actions against them. Agape love is a unique love, more important to humankind than anything else, for though everything else will pass away, only God and His love are eternal.

Relationship: Love and Deliverance

Relationship, according to *Oxford Pocket American Dictionary* means:

1. The fact or state of being related.
2. A connection or association (especially sexual) between two people.
3. A condition or character due to being related.
4. Kinship.

What is one thing that everyone wants, needs and is looking for, from the time a child is born until the time of death? It is a *"loving relationship"* that results in:

- knowing that someone loves and cares for you
- receiving attention and being listened to and accepted just as you are
- having someone to stand by you
- being loved without having to prove yourself or justify yourself

This is the kind of love that all humans need and desire—a loving, caring, Godly relationship, birthed out of the agape love of God and an extension of the love of God. It is attained only by the power of the indwelling and infillings of the Holy Spirit.

The reality is that very few people in this world actually love that way. Many of God's people are feeling lonely unloved and sad; but in Christ, we can all experience this kind of loving relationship when we are delivered and set free. God's love is a free gift to us, and He desires that we be free to love and be loved.

The dictionary defines "love" as:

1. "An intense affection for another person based on familiar or personal ties" (familiar spirits and soul ties).
2. Sexual passion.

3. Sexual relations.

4. A beloved one; a sweetheart.

In most cases, "intense affection" is derived from a sexual attraction to a person. People tend to love people in this erotic (*eros*) way when they are attracted to them and make them feel good. The key phrase here is "based on"; this implies a conditional love—based on something the person has or does. It is a love of someone because they fulfill a certain condition. People often say to each other, "I love you because you *are* this or that," or "I love you because you *do* this or that." This type of love is not agape; it is is conditional and based on feelings and emotions that can change from one moment to the next.

Let's turn to the other dictionary definition of love, associated with "intense affection," "familiar spirits," and "soul ties." Many Christians desire to know God in a deeper way and to exemplify a godly love toward their fellow man. However, they know that they have emotional or spiritual hindrance in their lives from past affectionate relationships. The question for the minister of deliverance is how such believers can be set free from them? Love that is emotionally fed through conditions and feelings generated from and associated with natural or carnal relationships is spiritually unhealthy. This is a doorway that the enemy uses to gain ground.

These are "Spirits of Affinity," which suggests a natural attraction to a person or thing, and they fall into the four categories listed and defined below:

- **Soul Ties**—This is a spirit that has the power to attract and unite. It creates a force of connectedness between two entities for the purpose of reinforcing divine or diabolical intents. The enemy, however, can pervert these

God-given relationships to fulfill his destructive plans and purposes.

• **Familiar Spirits**—Familiar spirits are very similar in nature to spirits of divination. They are demonic agents whose main assignment is to become well-acquainted with a person—as a secret agent; they are responsible for satanic surveillance and carrying out covert vigilante activities designed to steal, kill, and destroy. They gather information on the person to whom they are assigned and pass it along to another spirit for future use. Familiar spirits know the person they are assigned to so well that they can even imitate him or her. This ability produces deception in séances of talking to dead relatives and friends. The ability to contact spirits is often passed from one generation to the next within receptive families. The word "familiar" comes from the root word "family."

• **Spirits of Inheritance/Generational Curses**—Biologists, sociologists, and psychologists agree that there lies within man the propensity for certain behaviors, tendencies, traits, weaknesses, strengths, and habits that are peculiar to particular families. Exodus 20:5 says:

"I the Lord thy God am a jealous God, visiting the iniquity of the fathers upon the children unto the third and fourth generation."

This scripture lets us know that we are dealing with intergenerational spirits. The effects of generational curses are recorded in Deuteronomy 28:45-46:

"Moreover all these curses shall come upon you and pursue and overtake you, until you are destroyed, because you did not obey the voice of the Lord your

God to keep His commandments and His statutes which He commanded you. And they shall be upon you for a sign and a wonder, and on your descendants forever."

- **Unholy Association**—Satan employs principalities and spirits whose special assignment is to identify and mobilize other principalities and spirits to form confederations. Here we see that deliverance can be both simple and complex, depending on the amount of emotional, physical, mental, or spiritual damage has been done in the a person's relationships. Deliverance Ministry is not a cure-all, but deliverance is one part of the overall equation in God's salvation plan. When Christians have explored the different medical and psychological areas available to them and find no relief, deliverance and inner healing should be considered. Christians who have been wounded in the soul areas of their lives struggle with relationships and are bound by emotional issues that often had adverse effects in various spheres of life. This is especially common as a sequel to abuse and rejection. This makes it hard to express or receive the love of God and others, and therefore hinders the agape loving relationships that all humans desire.

Deliverance Revealed in the Bible

Deliverance in the Old Testament

God's revelation in the Old Testament serves to make the truths of the New Testament come alive in the believer's Christian walk. The five books of Moses in the Old Testament (Genesis, Exodus, Leviticus, Numbers, and Deuteronomy) are sometimes considered merely as historical accounts of great events. In truth, however, these books reveal biblical truths about how God operates as the great Deliverer in the lives of His people (i.e., Christians). These books of the Old Testament reveal the love, power, and grace of God and His redemption plan for His people. Once we realize that God's way of working in the lives of Christians today is fundamentally the same as His way of working in the lives of Adam, Abraham, Moses, David, Job, the Prophets, and others. God does not change. The desire to redeem, provide, heal, and deliver His people is as alive today as it was in the books of the Old Testament.

Deliverance is both rescue (or redemption) and the agent of such rescue. Scripture teaches that God's goal in history is to rescue people from the curse of sin, death, Satan, and hell. The Old Testament depicts God as delivering his chosen people from Egyptian slavery, from Assyrian and Babylonian captivity, and from oppression at the hands of various Palestinian tribes. To

Christians those deliverances foreshadow the coming of Jesus Christ as supreme deliverer.

The Old Testament concept of deliverer is expressed in a Hebrew word for "next of kin." A close relative was responsible to aid an individual in distress and to redeem him or her from slavery. God sent deliverance when His people were in danger, or God Himself acted as deliverer, uniquely and forcefully, as in the exodus from Egypt (Exodus 3:7-8). This "next of kin" is a type of the Deliverance Minister who acts through agency and authority of Jesus, the Deliverer, to release captives from bondage.

Deliverance: Genesis

Genesis is the book of beginnings that charts the origins of the earth as well as the origins of mankind's need for deliverance (salvation). The creation of man is established—as well as the fall and the introduction of sin in the "good" creation, his spiritual death , new beginning (the flood), human government and language. Genesis also introduces the existence of demonic beings. Demons and demonic activity are present in the book of Genesis (the beginning). They are there as fallen angels, as disembodied spirits of a pre-Adamic race (Genesis 1:2), or as the result of the cohabitation of angelic beings with antedeluvian women (Genesis 6:1-4). In Genesis, an unidentified being called the serpent introduced spiritual warfare into the human experience.

Genesis is about God's purpose and plan for His creation. It reveals the person and nature of God. Then sin enters the world, and Satan is unmasked in the fall of man, the effects of sin, the Messianic promise, the warfare between the seed of Satan and the seed of the woman, and the need of mankind for deliverance as well as a Deliverer.

Identify - Confront - Cast out

Deliverance: Exodus

Exodus reveals God's answer to man's need and His remedy for man's sin. It is God's design for deliverance; the pattern is laid out with lessons to man of what deliverance is. We see the pattern: God's people are in bondage, so God raises up a human agent through who He will deliver them out of the hand of Pharaoh. Moses himself was saved from death as a baby only to be raised up in the house of Pharaoh to be the deliverer of Israel. In Exodus God reveals Himself to Moses and assures him that He was aware of the cruel afflictions of His people and had heard their cries. Then he told Moses of His plan to send him to Egypt to deliver his people from their bondage.

In chapters 3-12 we see spiritual warfare in the form of a power encounter of "God" and the gods of Egypt. To bring Israel back (deliver, rescue) to the true God, they needed God to demonstrate that His power was greater than the power of all the gods of Egypt. In Exodus 4:29-31, we see the Israelites' responding to the power of demonstrations.

> *"Moses and Aaron brought together all the elders of the Israelites, an Aaron told them everything the Lord has said to Moses. He also performed the signs before the people, and they believed. And when they heard that the Lord was concerned about them and had seen their misery, they bowed down and worshiped."*

Unbeknownst to Pharaoh, he had established the challenge and the main ingredient of a "power encounter" when he intentionally mocked God.

Exodus 5:2 states: *"Who is the Lord that I should obey him and let Israel go? I do not know the Lord and I will not let Israel go."* The power demonstrations begin when God sets the stage in Exodus 6:1, where God said, *"Now you shall see what I will do to Pharaoh; because of my mighty hand, he will let them go, because of my mighty hand, he will drive them out of his country."*

God issued the power challenge to the gods of Egypt. As Pharaoh responded with his own challenge, God demonstrated that He was going to judge the gods of Egypt. Exodus 12:12 states:

> *"On that same night I will pass through Egypt and strike down every firstborn, both men and animals and I will bring judgment on all the gods of Egypt. I am the Lord."*

God allowed the magicians to match power with power and miracle with miracle with Moses and Aaron. This is the only record in the scriptures of a power encounter in which the servants of the no-gods were allowed to duplicate the power demonstrations of the servants of God. We realize, however, that this only served to emphasize the absolute power of God Almighty. For the Israelites to be delivered from death, a lamb with no defects had to be killed and its blood placed on the doorframes of each home. The lamb was a substitute for the person who would have died in the plagues. At this point the people clearly understood that an innocent life had to be sacrificed in their stead.

Deliverance: Joshua

The next major spiritual warfare encounter in the Old Testament is with the no-gods of the pagan nations surrounding Israel after Israel's entrance into the promised land. Joshua told the Israelites to throw away their foreign gods and man-made idols (Joshua 24). The foreign gods form the major spiritual warfare set against Israel throughout the rest of the Old Testament. God spoke to His people through Joshua and instructed them to choose to serve the Lord God rather than the false gods of their forefathers beyond the river (the Euphrates) and in Egypt.

The false gods they might have served included:

- The gods of Mesopotamia in Babylon (beyond the river); these included gods of war, fertility (Dagan, god of the Philistines), sexual love, cult prostitutes, ceremonial sexual encounters, and others.

- The gods of Egypt (whom their forefathers had worshipped during the Egyptian bondage); many of the Egyptian gods were in animal form or human form with animal heads. Deadly animals—snakes (cobras), scorpions, crocodiles, and others—were associated with gods and worshipped. Also male and female nudity was common in the idols, sexual organs were grossly exaggerated in various depictions; this was common among the pagan religions of Egypt.

- The gods of the Amorites (in whose land they lived); the Amorites included all the people of Canaan. These people served Baal, the greatest of the Canaanite gods. Baal means "owner, master, lord, husband." Baal was viewed as the god of life and land, the god of weather and the nature gods and was responsible for child sacrifice. Baal and the local Baals were the chief deities in the land of Canaan.

Joshua made it clear in chapter 24:14 that he made a commitment to the Lord God, and he vowed to live up to it. The Jews slowly learned the consequences of serving foreign gods.

Deliverance: Job

The book of Job begins with Satan, who is behind all the sufferings and losses of Job. Satan, not God, is directly responsible for all of the attacks on Job. Noteworthy is the fact that Satan was also the cause of the natural disasters that befell Job as well as the sudden death of all of Job's children. All this havoc, however, was not without the permission of God. Job 1:1-2:13 describes the events that led up to the sufferings of Job.

Satan appeared on the scene, and the Lord asks him, *"Have you noticed my servant Job?"* God then begins to describe Job: He is the finest man in all the earth, a man of integrity, who fears God and will have nothing to do with evil.

Satan's replies, "But take away everything he has and he will surely curse you to your face!" At that, God gave Satan permission to tempt Job with sufferings. Another encounter between the Lord and Satan leads to the physical suffering of Job:

> *"The Lord said to Satan, "Very well, then, everything he has is in your hands, but on the man himself do not lay a finger." (Job 1:12)*

> *"Satan replied, 'A man will give all he has for his own life. But stretch out your hand and strike his flesh and bones, and he will surely curse you to your face.' The Lord said to Satan, 'Very well, then, he is in your hands; but you must spare his life.'" (Job 2:4-6)*

Deliverance is available to everybody. Often the word "deliverance" refers to deliverance or release from satanic forces, such as drug addiction, alcoholism, or prostitution. But deliverance is not only for addicts and prostitutes; it is available to everyone, for everyone is engaged in the spiritual warfare against Satan and the demons.

"For our struggle is not against flesh and blood, but against the rulers, against the authorities, against the powers of this dark world, against the spiritual forces of wickedness in the air." (Ephesians 6:10-12)

Deliverance: Psalms

The book of Psalms is the book of the Old Testament with the most common use of the words *salvation* and *saves*. The contexts in which they are used indicate that salvation is deliverance from one's enemies. Most often "salvation" is spoken of in Psalms to refer to deliverance of the nation of Israel from her enemies. Occasionally, it refers to deliverance of the person from his or her enemies. Many of the Psalms speak of man as blessed—fallen and redeemed by God. The Psalmist often cries out to God in anguish and despair as he discovers the power of prayer and praise as God rescues his people in the midst of trouble. God is depicted here most often as our faithful Deliverer.

• **Deliverance from Enemies**

"The Lord is my rock and my fortress and my deliverer; My God my strength, in whom I will trust; my shield and the horn of my salvation, my stronghold. I will call upon the Lord, who is worthy to be praised; so shall I be saved from my enemies." (Psalm 18:2-3)

This Psalm is almost a duplicate of 2 Samuel 22 and may have been written toward the end of David's life.

• **Deliverance from Wicked (Nations and Individuals)**

"Do not take me away with the wicked and with the workers of iniquity, who speak peace to their neighbors, but evil in their hearts. Give them according to their deeds and according to the wickedness of their endeavors; give them according to the work of their

hands; render to them what they deserve." (Psalm 28:3-4)

The nations that were Israel's enemies were wicked. Thus, deliverance from the wicked is a closely related and often synonymous idea to that of deliverance from enemies. In Psalm 28:8-9, David refers to God as *"the saving refuge of His anointed. Save Your people, and bless Your inheritance."*

• **Deliverance from Trouble**

The second most frequent type of salvation in the Psalms is deliverance from troubles in this life. For example:

"Now consider this, you who forget God, lest I tear you in pieces, and there be none to deliver: Whoever offers praise glorifies Me; and to him who orders his conduct aright I will show the salvation of God." (Psalm 50:22-23)

The salvation or deliverance is spelled out earlier in the context:

"Call upon Me in the day of trouble; I will deliver you, and you shall glorify Me."

God provides salvation in the day trouble. Similarly Psalm 91:15-16 declares:

"He shall call upon Me, and I will answer him; I will be with him in trouble; I will deliver him and honor him. With long life I will satisfy him, and show him my salvation."

God saves those who call upon Him from troubles in this life.

"May the Lord answer you in the day of trouble... May He grant you according to your heart's desire, and fulfill all your purpose. We will rejoice in your salvation, and in the name of our God we will set up

our banners! May the Lord fulfill all your petitions."
(Psalm 20:1, 4-5)

Salvation from troubles is a common theme in the Psalms.

- **Deliverance of the Poor and Needy from their Afflictions**

This is a special type of salvation from troubles. Specifically, on some occasions, the psalmist speaks of the salvation of the poor and needy from their afflictions.

> *"For the oppression of the poor, for the sighing of the needy, now I will arise, says the Lord; "I will set him in the safety (salvation) for which he yearns." (Psalm 12:5)*

> *"Let all those who seek You rejoice and be glad in You; let such as love Your salvation say continually, 'The Lord be magnified! But I am poor and needy; Yet the Lord thinks upon me. You are my help and my deliverer; do not delay, O my God.'" (Psalm 40:16-17)*

Surely, if David (a man after God's own heart) could call himself "poor and needy," then all believers are poor and in need of some type or deliverance from our afflictions, whether they acknowledge it or not.

Deliverance in the New Testament

Deliverance: Gospels

The Gospels reveal the person of Jesus Christ from His birth to His death and resurrection. They present His life and ministry and teachings. The Gospel accounts clearly serve to demonstrate that Christianity is more than a religion—it is a relationship. Bishop Noel Jones, in Battle for the Mind, wrote that "it is in the Gospels that man meets God, face-to-face. The One who lived in the face of God now comes to exegete (explain) God to man." Satan's opposing Jesus' ministry starts immediately after the heavens open, and God the Father speaks for all to hear that this is His "beloved Son" with whom He is "well pleased." Before Jesus starts to preach, teach, heal, and cast out demons Satan makes his move, justifying his title as the tempter. "Then Jesus was led up by the Spirit into the wilderness to be tempted by the devil And after He had fasted forty days and forty nights, He then became hungry. And the tempter came and said to Him…" (Matthew 4:1-2)

Jesus overcame the devil with a strong rebuke—"Get thee behind Me Satan"—and quoting of scripture. The result was that "the devil left Him…." Deliverance in the Gospels is a demonstration of God's grace; Jesus proclaimed His gospel (good news) to the entire nation, from the respectable and noble to the least. All were called to submit to God's rule and invited to come and partake freely of the banquet He had spread (Luke 14:16-21). But the gift of salvation must be received if it is to be experienced. The gospel is more than a historical report of past events and the disclosing of doctrine.

Romans 1:16 states:

> *"For I am not ashamed of the gospel of Christ: for it is the 'Power of God' unto salvation to everyone that believeth; to the Jew first, and also to the Greek."*

Not only does the gospel of Christ bear witness to "the power of God"; it is the power of God—an expression of the power of Almighty God. This means that the gospel itself is a mighty work of God through His Holy Spirit, and God's purpose in exercising His power is to change people's lives, to liberate them from sin and death, and to reconcile them to Himself. This is deliverance unto salvation. The gospel has the power to affect the deliverance it announces and to impart the life it promises. If people are going to experience true deliverance, they must first hear and believe the gospel. The gospel cannot be restricted or restrained; it is the decisive place of encounter between the sinner and Almighty God, the great Deliverer.

In reading the Gospels, we see that the conflict between opposing forces—God and Satan (good and evil)—is the center of New Testament Christianity. Jesus was Satan's prime target. He was a marked man from conception. Satan used every opportunity to try to prevent Jesus from laying down His life for the sins of the world. He had major encounters with the demonic, and the way in which He dealt with them provides believers with an understanding of the whole Deliverance Ministry of Jesus. Not every type of demonic power is represented in the Gospels, but the principles Jesus used are clear. The Gospels record major physical attacks on Jesus' life because Jesus was an active threat to Satan and his kingdom.

In this section we will examine some of the major encounters Jesus had with demonic powers in the Synoptic Gospels (i.e., Matthew, Mark, and Luke).

- **Jesus' Encounter: In Nazareth** (Matthew 13:53-58; Mark 6:1-6; Luke 4:16-30)

The people of Nazareth knew Jesus and His family from childhood, so they had a problem believing the message of a neighbor who came to them as a prophet and challenged them to respond to spiritual truths. These people were too close to the family; they couldn't hear the message because they knew Jesus the man. Jesus went into the synagogue on the Sabbath to worship and began to teach, and many were astonished and others were offended. They viewed Jesus merely as the carpenter's son. They rejected His authority and thought of Him as one of them. Jesus said a prophet is never honored in his own home (Mark 6:4).

As He stood up read the scriptures from (Isaiah 61:1):

> *"The Spirit of the Lord is upon me… to bring good news to the poor. He has sent me to proclaim liberty to the captives and recovery of sight to the blind, to set free the oppressed and announce that the time has come when the Lord will save his people."*

There was a direct power encounter between Jesus and the demons that motivated the crowd. Satan attempted to incite the spirit of murder on the hearts of the people. Jesus moved on.

- **Jesus' Encounter: At Capernaum** (Mark 1:21-28; Luke 4:31-37)

Jesus was speaking in the synagogue, and a man tormented by an unclean spirit screamed out with aloud voice, questioning Jesus, "What do your want with us [more than one]? Are you here to destroy us [recognized the power]?" Jesus rebuked the demons and they came out, and as they came out they acknowledged Jesus, for they knew who He was. The people were amazed and wondered what a word this was because of the *authority and power* possessed by Jesus.

- **Jesus' Encounter: At Simon's House and After** (Matthew 8:14-17; Mark 1:29-34; Luke 4:38-41).

Simon's wife's mother had a high fever and was looking for Jesus. The scripture tells us exactly what Jesus did. Jesus discerned that the illness was not merely physical but that there was a spiritual power (cause) behind the physical symptom. So Jesus addressed the spirit of infirmity and cursed the fever and ordered it to go. And the Bible says it left *immediately*, and her strength was restored and she got up and began serving the others.

- **Jesus' Encounter: With a mute man** (Matthew 9:32)

  The senses are vulnerable to demonic attack and in some cases they can even appear to be controlled by demons. This text shows the individual cases in the Gospels, and the fact that not every case has the same root cause. Demons can produce symptoms that are perceived as physical but are, in fact, caused by the presence of a demon. Matthew's account of the reason why this mute man could not speak is simple and graphic—because he had a demon! As soon as Jesus drove the demon out the man, he started talking *(not all muteness is demonic)*.

- **Jesus and the Disciples: Encounter with the Epileptic Boy** Matthew 17:14-21; Mark 9:14-29; Luke 9:37-43).

  While Jesus was away an epileptic boy was brought to the disciples and they could not heal him. The father complained to Jesus, and Jesus rebuked the foul spirit and charged him not to enter again. The disciples questioned Jesus as to why they couldn't cast the demon out and Jesus informed them that kind only comes out by faith, through prayer and fasting" Jesus Himself said to the disciples that it was a serious case of demonization, not amenable to the usual manner of casting out demons. Deliverance was such an integral part of Jesus' ministry that the father and the disciples were surprised and wondered why the demon did not respond to the command of the disciple's authority.

- **Jesus' Encounter: With the Gadarene Demoniac** (Matthew 8:28-34; Mark 5:1; Luke 8:26-39). The goal of demons is to control the humans they inhabit; Jesus' goal was to deliver people from sin and Satan's control. Herein is the crux of the spiritual struggle between Jesus and Satan. The demons realized they were no match for the power of Jesus. This Gadarene man was inhabited (possessed) by an army of perhaps 6,000 demons at one time, and they recognized who Jesus was. The Bible says that the man ran and fell down on his knees in front of Jesus and began to plead with Jesus by God (the Father) not to torture them and not to send them out of the area but rather to send them into the swine. Evil spirits can do horrible things to the human body and cause much destruction and torment (in leaving as well as remaining). Retaliation, transference, and backlash are some of the trauma inflicted by departing spirits.

The more demonized a person is, the greater the demonic powers and supernatural strength in the victim's body.

This man displayed all of the effects of major demonic possession:

a. **Supernatural strength:** he tore chains and broke irons from his feet.
b. **Cutting and screaming:** he would cry out and cut himself with stones.
c. **Nakedness:** he wore no clothing.
d. **Hung around the tombs:** was at home among the dead.
e. **Could not be bound:** must be cast out.

Had Jesus not consented to allow the demons to enter the swine, the effects on the man would have been fatal, with the legion of demons tearing at his flesh as they left. They went into the swine, and the man was set-free and wanted to follow Jesus. But Jesus declined and told him: "Go back home and tell what God has done for you." This story demonstrates why it is so important to recognize evil activity and to stay away from it. Curiosity about demons or involvement with demonic forces or the occult is forbidden (Deuteronomy 18:10-2). Satan is behind the occult, and God does not want His children to have anything to do with it. Even today people are fascinated by horoscopes, fortune-telling, witchcraft, and cults.

Deliverance: Acts of the Apostles

Christianity was quickly spreading across the Roman Empire through preaching, healing, and deliverance. In the book of Acts we realize that a great move under the anointing of the Holy Spirit was the normal pattern for ministry; and it was the status quo in the earliest Church. All of the warfare in the book of Acts focuses on Christian leaders and their encounters with Satan and his evil forces. Satan is not mentioned until Acts 5, but we can be sure that he was present from the beginning. Crowds of people came from the towns around Jerusalem, bringing the sick and those vexed with evil spirits, and they all were healed (Acts 5:16). There were various acts of deliverance during that time.

Ephesus was the most important city in Asia Minor in the first century. But it was also plagued with occult practices. Paul set out to minister the truth of Jesus to this major population center of Satan's earthly kingdom. Paul was the most educated of the apostles. His ministry was modeled on the ministry of Jesus. Teaching and healing were the basis of his work. God performed unusual miracles through Paul. At one point handkerchiefs and aprons he had used were given to the sick and their diseases and evil spirits were driven away (Acts 19:11-12).

Sceva was a Jewish High Priest whose seven sons were Jewish exorcists who traveled around the area attempting to drive evil spirits out of people (Acts 19:13-14). They witnessed Paul at work and were impressed with the power and authority he displayed. When they saw people being healed and delivered, they thought they knew exactly what to do. When they addressed a man to deliver him in the "Name of Jesus whom Paul preaches," the demons saw nothing of the Holy Spirit or Jesus in the sons of Sceva, and they responded by violently overpowering all seven and tore off their clothes and sent them running for their lives.

PART II

Essential Tools for Deliverance Ministers

CHAPTER 5

Fundamentals of Christian Deliverance

FUNDAMENTAL MEANS "basic, primary, elementary, and essential." The fundamentals of Christian deliverance deals with "basic deliverance" as it relates to Christian living. In the narrow sense, spiritual warfare is a result of God's redemptive plan and process being carried out in the various dimensions of Christian living. The Christian's persistent engagement in spiritual warfare involves the issue of sanctification and constant conflict in the mind (which is the main theater of spiritual warfare). Many are attacked with temptations, evil thoughts, rejection, bitterness, unforgiveness, and other sins. Sins that come from within are *personal*, and thus warfare with the flesh. Sin is also *social*, and can come from sources outside of the flesh, in which case the warfare is with the world or worldview. And, finally, sin can come from *supernatural* sources, in which case the warfare is with evil spirits. Ultimately, Satan is the source of all of the Christian's sin problems. Satan's methods of demonic attacks are through the flesh, the world, and his evil spirits.

The roots of this cosmic conflict between God and Satan extend back to a time before humans were created, and it took place in the heavenlies. Within the Kingdom of God, Lucifer (Satan) was one of the highest ranking angels in the angelic hierarchy—and was perhaps above even the archangels Michael and

Gabriel. The point is that Satan's kingdom is highly organized and very much purposed to do his evil deeds undetected and unchallenged. Satan is a highly intelligent being and is very aware of how the Kingdom of God operates. He knows all the legal and illegal bases for footholds in believers' lives. His power and misuse of power, however, are corrupt. His power is limited and, as with all power, it is subject ultimately to God. Satan's time on earth and his boundaries are all set by God.

Basic Deliverance

Basic deliverance deals with life from a Christian perspective. Life for the Christian is a continual battle of evil forces from the flesh, the world, and the devil. The notion that once a person becomes a Christian he or she is immune to struggles is not only untrue but harmful. The truth is that once a person receives Jesus as Lord over his life, the struggles intensify. As a result of receiving Jesus Christ as Lord, however, the believer also receives power and authority over the enemy.

One of the believer's best defenses is to know the enemy and understand his purposes and tactics to know how to thwart his attempts to take advantage of the men and women of God. Paul wrote in 2 Corinthians 2:11: *"Lest Satan should take advantage of us, for we are not ignorant of his devices."*

It is important for believers to realize that sin, life experiences, and inheritance (or generational curses) provide entry points for demonic activity.

Thus, Deliverance Ministers must learn to make use of the two primary methods of detecting evil spirits:

(1) *By the unction of the Holy Spirit, through the revelatory gifts of the Spirit.* There are times when any one or all of

the following three revelation gifts are operating in order to bring deliverance.

- **Word of Wisdom:** A revelation of the future under the anointing of God.

- **Word of Knowledge:** A revelation of a fact that can only be revealed supernaturally.

- **Discerning of Spirits:** The discerning of the human spirit (good and bad), as revealed supernaturally by the Holy Spirit. This gift enables the Deliverance Minister to discern (e.g., by looking at a person) whether he or she is telling the truth.

(2) *By observing what the evil spirits are doing to a person.* Evidence of demonic activity is often present in the following areas of life and functioning:

- **Emotional:** Most commonly through rejection, feeling unwanted and unloved.

- **Mental:** Mental anguish, torment, procrastination, indecision, compromise, confusion, doubt, rationalization and loss of memory.

- **Physical/Health:** Diseases and physical afflictions due to spirits of infirmity. There is a close relationship between deliverance and healing.

- **Religious:** Involves any degree of religious error that can open the door for demons.

  - False religions, pagan religions, mind sciences (including interests in yoga exercises, karate, etc.)

  - Christian cults, Jehovah's Witnesses, Christian Science

- Occult and Spiritism, séances, witchcraft, magic, Ouija boards, astrology, divination etc.

- **Sexually:** Recurring unclean thoughts and acts regarding sex. These include fantasy sex, masturbation, lust, perversions, homosexuality, fornication, adultery, incest, promiscuousness, whore-mongering, and harlotry.

Rejection

Many emotional problems manifest in common and familiar patterns that Deliverance Ministers can learn to detect through observation. The most common evidence of satanic oppression is rejection. Perhaps the reason is that Satan was rejected by God, never to be accepted into the Kingdom of God again. And mankind through the grace of God and the blood of Jesus has the option to escape and be delivered and forgiven of all sin and accepted into the Kingdom of God. Rejection manifests in various ways. A person can be rejected intentionally or unintentionally.

- Rejection is something that can be active or passive in nature. Rejection will affect most people in one way or another at some point between conception and death.

- Rejection in many cases is received at the time of conception or through the circumstances surrounding conception. If a child is conceived out of wedlock, incest, adultery, rape, or as a result of anger, rejection can be received without any knowledge on the part of the recipient.

- Rejection may be received while the baby is still in the mother's womb.

- Rejection can be received by a baby not bonded to its mother after birth.

- Rejection can always be found in an adopted child.
- Rejected parents produce rejected children.
- Rejection by parents for not being of the desired gender.
- Rejection because of a birth defect, or a physical disability secondary to an accident or disease.
- Rejection caused by speech impediments, stuttering, or inability to correctly pronounce certain words.
- Rejection caused by parental cruelty, alcoholism.
- Rejection caused by being made to feel inferior.
- Rejection caused by being excluded by siblings, friends, or teachers.
- Rejection caused by death, divorce, or unfaithfulness in a marriage.
- Rejection caused by being let down by people who had been trusted and relied on.

Symptoms of rejection include an insatiable desire for physical love and assurances of self-worth. The roots of rejection produce many aggressive attitudes, and rejection oftentimes is motivated by the *fear of rejection* (i.e., the person who fears rejection engages in behaviors, such as control and manipulation, that lead others to reject him). This is a constant need to avoid being rejected again.

Bitterness

Bitterness is manifest in the manner in which a person handles emotional hurt, mental pain, or resentment. Bitterness manifests under many other spirits, such as rebellion, perversion, rejection, etc. Hebrews 12:15 states: *"Looking diligently lest any man fail of the grace of God: lest any root of bitterness spring up trouble you, and thereby many be defiled."* A bitter person does not care about the person toward whom he is bitter.

The characteristics of a person who harbors bitterness in the heart are:

(1) Ungratefulness/ingratitude

(2) Holding grudges and an unforgiving spirit

(3) Stubbornness and undesirable attitudes

(4) Constant complaining

(5) Harshly critical

(6) Extreme mood swings

The fruit of bitterness are anger, wrath, slander, hatred, and malice (or desire to see another suffer).

Unforgiveness

Bitterness manifests commonly in the "sin" of unforgiveness. Unforgiveness occurs when one refuses to forgive an offense without punishment or retribution. It is common in the attitude "don't get mad, get even."

(1) Unforgiveness clings to the sins of someone else's past and brings them into the present of the one offended.

(2) It affects other relationships of the offended person.

(3) It causes division in the Body of Christ and brings about jealousy, envy, and strife.

(4) The root cause of unforgiveness is pride.

(5) Unforgiveness can cause one to commit the sin of omission by failing to forgive.

(6) Unforgiveness can cause one to become a stumbling block and opens the door for Satan to gain advantage in one's life and relationships.

When people have been seriously hurt they have the choice to forgive through an act of their own will. Healing and deliverance comes many times through forgiveness more than any other spiritual discipline.

Rebellion

Rebellion is a spirit related to the spirit of pride and occurs whenever one refuses to submit to the authority of God (John 14:23). Jesus said that obedience to his commandments is a way of expressing our love to Him. It is also our greatest means of protection from the enemy. Many times attitudes and habits can't be broken through repenting, cleansing and will-power. This is an indication that a strongman may be present and deliverance is needed to break this yoke of rebellion.This is a spirit that leads one to do wicked things that are against God. Rebellion says in so many words, "I am equal to God in wisdom and knowledge." This is the prideful attitude that causes one to refuse to listen to the word or voice of God.

> *"For rebellion is as the sin of witchcraft, and stubbornness is as iniquity and idolatry. Because thou has rejected the word of the Lord, he has also rejected thee from being king." (1 Samuel 15:23)*

Deliverance: In Spiritual Areas

Deliverance in spiritual areas is one of man's greatest needs. The outward appearance of a person (i.e., the public persona he portrays) is not necessarily an accurate reflection of inward person. Thus, Deliverance Ministers must learn to detect incongruence between a person's outward presentation and inner life. The spiritual-man (inner-man) does not match the physical-outer-man (flesh). The Apostle Paul was all too aware of the struggle. In Romans 7:22-25 he writes:

> *"For I delight in the law of God after the inward man: But I see another law in my members, warring against the law of my mind, and bringing me into captivity to the law of sin which is in my members O wretched man that I am! Who shall deliver me from the body of this death? thank God through Jesus Christ our Lord. So then with the mind I myself serve the law of God: but with the flesh the law of sin."*

The Spirit of God resides in our inward man, which is the regenerated spiritual areas of the soul that include the unseen realm of the mind, emotions, and will. The inward man wears the flesh as a coat or covering. One of the reasons spiritual attacks cause so much affliction to believers and non-believers is that they cannot be seen by the victims themselves.

For example, when someone expresses hearing the voices or the demands of demons, the Deliverance Minister cannot see or hear what the person is experiencing, yet he knows it is a real experience. Some such attacks are so severe that the victims end up in psychiatric hospitals, have emotional breakdowns, or commit suicide. Spiritual attacks can also affect a person's soul. This is the area Satan desires to control (Nee, 1977).

The Mind

According to the Hebrew way of thinking revealed in the Old Testament there is no specific word for "mind." Several Hebrew words address the human mind including *nepes* (Genesis 23:8) and *ruah* (Genesis 26:35). The Hebrew word most often used for "mind" is *nephesh*, the etymological root of which denotes to breathe or refresh oneself. In the broad sense of the text, the "mind" includes the entire intellectual and cognitive functions of one's inner life, considered the heart or soul of a person. This being the case, the translators of the English versions have used other words as the context suggests, such as soul, spirit, or heart. The Greek concept of "mind" is from the word *phrones,* and it means *to set one's mind on a thing.* There are several other words, however, that signify the human cognitive capacity or spiritual-rational-intellectual function, especially for perceiving spiritual realities.

The mind (psychological) is the spiritual organ that generates thought and processes all incoming information whereas the brain is the physical (physiological) expression of the mind that operates like a super computer in storing information and carrying out the routine functions that control the body. The mind is equipped to know, think, imagine, understand, and remember. The mind is what enables us to recognize and evaluate situations and circumstances in our lives. Whether right or wrong, good or bad, all things spiritual and carnal begin with the mind. According to Bishop Noel:

> "The carnal mind always listens to the desires of the
> flesh, while the spiritual mind is concerned about
> how the human spirit relates to God" (cited in
> Murphy, 2006).

This is a apt analogy because the mind is engaged before thought is generated; the mind does not sleep or rest. The mind serves to protect people from themselves and their environment. It tells the body to function, breathe, think, move, etc. The mind makes one aware of dangers around in the environment that may threaten physical, mental, or spiritual well-being. This is why the mind is the where spiritual warfare is waged. Whatever controls the mind controls the person—the life, soul, appetite, and personality. Colossians 3:2 states, "*You have to set your mind on things above, not on things on the earth.*"

Paul put it this way in (Romans 8:6-7):

> "*For to be carnally minded (sensual, sinful, fleshly, and worldly) is death, but to be spiritually minded (connected and controlled by the Spirit of Christ) is life and peace. Because the carnal mind is enmity against God; for it is not subject to the law of God, nor indeed can be.*"

This is why believers are *transformed by the renewing of our minds* (Romans 12:2) to be more like Christ, which means having the mind of Christ Jesus (Philippians 2:5-8). The mind is where the transformation takes place in the renewing process, as believers develop a personal relationship with God and the Holy Spirit works on transforming the mind to a renewed state. To change one's mind is to change one's life; this impacts the spiritual life as well as the physical life.

The Emotions

Emotions are composed of sensual or instinctive feelings such as love, fear, joy, and sorrow. This causes us to act without conscious intentions or respond instinctively to events that are going on around us. Emotions affect us through:

- **Body:** Our response to a sudden loud noise may be fear.
- **Mind:** The satisfaction of creating something beautiful can give one the feeling of pleasure.
- **Will:** A bad decision may lead to distress.
- **Spirit:** a spiritual experience can bring one joy.

There are different sources of emotional pain such as abandonment, verbal abuse, sexual abuse, or physical violence that cause people to hide their real feelings as a survival technique for coping with emotional devastating experiences. God does not intend that His people remain in emotional pain because of ignorance. The availability of the healing and Deliverance Ministry of Jesus Christ clearly bring emotional healing and deliverance to the damaged lives of believers. The highest expression of emotion is experienced when the spirit, soul, and body are in perfect relationship with God. In some branches of the Church, emotional experiences is not considered as "real spirituality." God, however, created humans in His image, with emotions, for a purpose. Deliverance ministers must recognize emotional reality and help others bring their emotions to the Lord for healing. If not healed damaged emotions can devastate one's life and relationships. Emotion wounds need healing as surely as do physical wounds. Jesus died that believers may be healed and delivered in the area of their emotions as well as in all other areas of life.

The Will

The will is the third principal aspect of the soul with which people make decisions. It is comprised of desires, wants, and proclivities, and the choices made in regard to those things. Careful analysis of the scriptures reveals that every temptation that Satan uses to entice humans is introduced through the mind. The Bible speaks of the spirit's being willing whereas the flesh is weak. This means if the flesh is not crucified, then the will can go awry. Temptation comes to man through the process of thought. Satan will use every trick to make our wills subject to the flesh rather than to the spirit.

Many people lack judgment and are incapable of making healthy decisions because they cannot resist strong temptations that overtake their will. The contest of the wills is to do right versus doing wrong, when doing wrong (sin) is in accordance with one's desire. Manipulating the will is one of Satan's primary tactics, for if he can assume control of a person's will he can wreak havoc to every area of his life. Healing for the emotions is possible, and deliverance is often necessary, but it does require a level of obedience that only the Holy Spirit can provide. Therefore, if Satan injures the spirit / soul of man the results will be worse than physical sickness. Proverbs 18:14 states: *"A man's spirit sustains him in sickness, but a crushed spirit who can bear?*

The four main demonic entry points from which Satan inflicts spiritual injuries are listed below with a description of the demonic operation in each:

- **Deception**—This deceptive tactic of Satan includes glorifying earthly riches or worldly pleasures such as money, power, fame, beauty, and knowledge. Another deceptive tactic is false teachings on spiritual warfare and deliverance. Some false teachings expose believers to the dark spirit world and enable their human spirits to see and hear demonic forces. These practices tap into the wrong spirit world and cause Christians to see or experience unpleasant demonic activities.

- **Ignorance**—Ignorance (or lack of knowledge) predisposes a person to Satan's deception and false doctrines. Hosea 4:6 states: *"My people are destroyed from lack of knowledge."* Lack of knowledge can be an open door for all sorts of dangerous beliefs and doctrines that are introduced as though they biblically-based and sound.

- **Sin**—Sin has the same consequences whether it is committed knowingly or unknowingly. Sins that injure the spirit include involvement in occult practices, sexual sins, unforgiveness, and parent-child conflicts. Sexual sins bear the fruit of bitterness, anger, rejection, humiliation, and worthlessness. Proverbs 6:32-33 states: *"But a man who commits adultery lacks judgment; whoever does so destroys himself. Blows and disgrace are his lot, and his shame will never be wiped away."*

- **Storms of Life**—Storms of life are unpleasant experiences that happen to a person through no fault of his own. These include living under constant negative and critical words; betrayal (by a loved one or a trusted person, or a leader); death of a loved one; physical or emotional abuse; living in an oppressive environment fraught with fear, rejection, false accusations; divorce experiences, trauma, severe accidents, physical or social challenges, physical appearance issues, racial, gender, and ethnic discrimination or abuse.

Depending on how the storms of life are handled, they can be assets which Satan uses to hinder believers from moving forward. All believers have some degree of spiritual scars and some open wounds from past experiences; however, it (1) the severity of the experiences, and (2) the response to them that will determine whether they have a negative or positive effect on one's present life. The degree of the effect of the scar or wounds varies from person to person, and in different areas of the inner spirit. Some experiences make believers stronger in areas of protecting themselves in future situations while others result in severe physical, mental, or emotional *dis*-ease.

Manifesting Mental/Psychological Effects:

- Recurring bad dreams, nightmares, the so-called incubus dreams.
- Recurring memories of a past hurt(s).

- Proneness to memory losses or distorted memories, selective negative memory—exaggerating the negatives while minimizing (or forgetting) the positives.
- Focus on faults of others and shifting blame.
- Hypercritical and even judgmental of others.
- Difficulty in forgiving some people.
- Either extremely overconfident (prideful and arrogant) even when heading the wrong way or extremely pessimistic and timid.
- Either obsessed with cleanliness and hygiene or slovenly and unclean.

Manifesting Emotional Effects:

- Either exceptionally withdrawn (extreme introversion) or exceptionally outgoing and people-pleaser (extreme extroversion).
- Inferiority complex, low self-esteem, poor self-concept.
- Exceptionally fearful, suspicious, and distrustful.
- Easily controlled by habits and compulsions such alcohol, drugs, food, television, and so on.
- Overwhelming feelings of guilt of some harm done (e.g., member of the armed services returning from war).
- Easily offended and angered; very sensitive.
- Difficulty giving and receiving love, praise, or approval.
- Both overprotective and possessive or extremely permissive and indulgent.

Manifesting Volitional Effects (the Will):

- Either excessive workaholic or completely unconcerned with work and industry, career, or obligations (sluggard, lazy, slothful).

- Either excessively perfectionistic (picky, fussy) or morally lax and disinterested (apathy) or unconcerned with doing what's right (chaotic).

- Either extremely cautious and insecure or extremely impulsive and reckless, prone to jumping from fire to fire.

- Either an extremely domineering personality ("control freak") or extremely weak-willed and easily manipulated.

- Exceptionally self-centered, arrogant, egotistical.

- Exceptionally defensive (even when wrong) and easily shifting blame on others.

- Both very stubborn and insensitive to correction ("bull-headed") or extremely impressionable, gullible, and helplessly dependent on others.

Other manifestations of spiritual injuries or attacks include fears or feelings of paranoia (suspicion that someone or something—the FBI, the government, neighbors, law enforcement—is watching the person) or sensing a presence behind or around the person. In some cases, people see evil spirits, hear voices, and have frequent nightmares or sexual encounters in dreams. For all such maladies and dis-ease, the Deliverance Minister must be mindful that spiritual deliverance is primarily the work of the Holy Spirit. The Holy Spirit is able to work in the inner most part of a person. He can overcome mindsets, emotions, twisted wills, and all such strongholds that people find difficult to give up or unwilling to let go of.

The Spirit transforms people by renewing their minds to value His ways above their own self-interests. The transforming of the mind directly affects all other areas of the spirits, including the emotions and volitions (the will). He works to restore believers to power, love, and a sound mind. He enables them to grow in having "the mind of Christ" that they might live under His influence and guidance. This begins the healing process to deliverance through the Holy Spirit of God. Philippians 2:5 states: *"Let this mind be in you which was also in Christ Jesus."*

Deliverance: In Social Areas

Deliverance in social areas is not a new concept. Social issues are the outward expression of the inner turmoil going on inside of a person in the guise of a controlling spirit, strongman, or master spirit. The deliverance of social abnormalities involves biblical principles that often baffle the minds of believers but not the enemy, who is well-informed in this area. James 4:7 states: *"Submit yourselves therefore to God. Resist the devil, and he will flee from you."* Let's examine the principles James set forth in this verse.

- **Submitting yourself to God:** This is a willful act of the soul; the devil knows when you are not submitted to God. Being saved does not necessarily imply being submitted to God. Being saved is activating Romans 10:9: *"That if you shall confess with your mouth the Lord Jesus, and shall believe in your heart that God has raised Him from the dead, you shall be saved."*

  Submitted, on the other hand, means to comply with the authority of His Word, to abide in His will, and commit one's life to Him and His control.

  - **Resist the devil:** The devil knows what your appetite calls for and he knows what tempts you.

- **He (the devil) will flee**: If you practice the first two principles, the Bible says the third will result: Satan will have to depart.

Deliverance in social behavior includes habits, desires, wants, and appetites in the Christian walk. 1 Corinthians 10:21 states: "*Ye cannot drink the cup of the Lord, and the cup of devils; ye cannot be partakers of the (Lord's Table and of the table of devils).* The principle here is that God will not share his children with the devil. Social deliverance is in part delivering that part of man that makes contact with the world. Being saved or born again is not being delivered; it is the beginning of a life of deliverance and healing. Deliverance is not always accomplished by casting out demons, identifying and listing curses, pleading the blood of Jesus on one's life, the collective petitions of a team of prayer warriors, and anointing with oil. These practices are very real and very relevant, but not all deliverances occur in that manner. Deliverance can be as simple as having a change of heart in an area of struggle that may seem to be a very simple act to one person yet very difficult to another.

For example, let's consider a case involving the spirit of lying. This Spirit of Lying is a master spirit or strongman under whose auspices come the influence of other spirits. It is noteworthy that *though every person who lies is not vexed with a lying spirit, every lie is a potential step toward acquiring the habit or appetite for lying.* Any one of the following is grounds for social deliverance:

- **Flattery**—false praise, compliments, adulation; "*He that goeth about as a talebearer revealeth secrets: therefore meddle not with him that flattereth with his lips*" (Proverbs 20:19).

- **Slander**—scandalous remarks; "*He that dideth hatred with lying lips, and he that uttereth a slander, is a fool*" (Proverbs 10:18).

- **False teachers**—False teachings are lies of Satan. False teachers invent false doctrines to get people to support them. The Word of God says; *"But there were false prophets also among the people, even as there shall be false teachers among you, who privily shall bring in damnable heresies, even denying the Lord that bought them, and bring upon themselves swift destruction" (2 Peter 2:1)* .

- **Gossip**—Gossiping or backbiting is a form of lying that hurts and even destroys innocent victims; just because the information is true does not mean it is right to broadcast it throughout the Church or community. *"But I say unto you that every idle word that men shall speak, they shall give account thereof in the day of judgment" (Matthew 12:36).*

- **Superstitions**—this is a very subtle but dangerous spirit, which says black cats crossing our paths or walking under ladders causes "bad luck." The Bible says nothing about "luck." *"But my God shall supply all your needs according to His riches in glory by Christ Jesus" (Philippians 4:19).*

Social deliverance is vital in Deliverance Ministry. The social bondages from which believers need to be delivered are various and sundry. Sometimes they are identified in symptoms from master spirits that have the potential to increase in severity. They affect our physical appearance, social demeanor, behaviors, and many outward mannerisms and actions. Believers are the representatives of Christ Jesus who make contact with the unsaved world. This is an area where social deliverance is necessary because the believer may be the only positive Christian example another person may come in contact with. We are social beings, and our social conduct is a declaration of our Christian walk. Common social areas of deliverance include: self-pity, inner hurts, brokenheartedness, drug use, consulting horoscopes, adultery, love of money, worldliness, excessive appetites, filthy mouth, filthy mind, coarse jokes, and others. When a believer is tempted in any of these areas, she or he or a Deliverance Minister must immediately bind the strongman and take dominion over the spirit aggressively and expeditiously.

When ministering to those who need social deliverance, Deliverance Ministers should help them practice the following spiritual disciplines:

- By prayer and fasting
- By spiritual cleansing
- By sanctification
- By spending quality study time in the Word of God
- By cultivating a great desire for inner peace
- By having an intense desire to obey God
- By having a reverence for the authority of God
- By having a repentant heart
- By having a refreshing of the Holy Spirit

Deliverance: In Financial Areas

1 Timothy 6:17-19 states:

> *"Charge them that are rich in this world, that they be not highminded, nor trust in uncertain riches, but in the living God, who giveth us richly all things to enjoy; That they do good, that they be rich in good works, ready to distribute, willing to communicate; Laying up in store for themselves a good foundation against the time to come, that they may lay hold on eternal life."*

The need for deliverance in financial areas is common. Issues arise not only from financial deficiency but because of man's tendency to trust in the riches of this world. This renders a person who seeks security and satisfaction on money vulnerable to disillusionment when calamity strikes through the storms and challenges of life. The evidence that the wealthy are at least as vulnerable to various life-challenges as those who are less wealthy is abundant. Truly money cannot buy happiness, health, or security. On the other hand, financial lack is one of the great concerns among afflicted believers. The Spirit of Affliction and the Spirit of Poverty are master spirits over financial afflictions. There are spirits is assigned to cause distress and disease by wreaking all sorts of major calamities in the life of believers. These are strongholds and should not be allowed to remain in place and go unchallenged; and all doors to establish them should be closed. Financial afflictions work in various ways—such as through deprivation, lack, debt, poverty, gambling, addiction, and so on. Many Christians are in serious financial straits, and some lack the basic means of life to support a family sufficiently. This is sometimes due to tragedies in life or through difficult situations.

The Bible provides principles that relate to financial and material well-being. God's principles do not promise to bring believers all that we may desire, but they will surely eliminate undue distress due to ignorance and lack of knowledge. Much financial affliction stems from a lack of discipline coupled with greed and lusts. When the flesh becomes loose and not subject or submitted to the Spirit of God, destructive attitudes can be as blatant as an idea of the pleasure of riches, fortune, and fame. On the other hand, it can be as subtle as a cursed word of poverty spoken over a family. Many times such a word is pronounced in jest, yet the effects can last for generations to come. The Bible declares that the power of our words, which have the ability to change our lives, homes, environment, communities, and so on.

Some teachers claim that tithing is not a requirement in the New Testament (New Covenant), and that we are free through Christ from those "Old Testament" religious rituals of the Law. It is beyond the scope of this study to argue the truth or error of that teaching, but the spiritual principle under which tithing and offering was established is still applicable today. The Bible does not stop speaking to us, and God does honor His Word, and spiritual principles will always be in place because they are eternal not temporary. God adds to the principles before He takes away from them. In the New Testament the limit on giving has changed. For example, the New Testament requires in that we offer our bodies as a living sacrifice (Romans 12:1). This is certainly more than a 10 percent tithe; this is giving everything to God for His use. We are urged in the Bible to be rich in good deeds, which stores up our treasures in heaven rather than on earth (Matthew 6:19-21).

Being obedient to God's Word is key to receiving financial deliverance. This truth is too often overlooked when a believer is in financial trouble but extremely important for any deliverance.

In Matthew 6:33, Jesus states:

> *"Seek first the kingdom of God, and His righteousness and all these things will be added unto you."*

This is putting the things of God first—before our personal interests and living a righteous life.

God has prescribed a way of escape for believers through His Word. The believer's job is to apply the principles and not look for worldly ways out of troubling situations (e.g., cutting back on tithing to "save" money), which in the end will only bring much grief and distress.

On the other hand, it is important to realize that other issues not related to lack of giving may be contributing to our financial troubles. Other hindrances, such as sins and disobedience in other areas of life may contribute to financial troubles as well. God disciplines out of His love for His children. It displeases Him when believers disobey His principles, financial or otherwise. His discipline is what enables believers to return to His ways when they go astray. When believers are disobedient, they rob God of what belongs to Him (Malachi 3: 8-9), and this puts nations, cities, churches, households, etc., under a curse. A whole nation can be under a curse because the head of the nation is walking in disobedience to God. This is true of churches, families, cities, etc. Withholding what is rightfully God's brings the curse of lack, creates deficiency, and promotes continual harassment from the devil through losses, an inferior quality of life, theft, financial disaster, and unnecessary burdens.

The most blessed countries, cities, churches, and households in the world are the ones that are not robbing God and in fact give the most to the kingdom of God. The curse is broken only when it is transformed into a blessing when they start giving. Money and material means are gifts, seeds for a material harvest. Material and financial harvest do not come from prayer because then only Christians would have material means. In the financial area, God personally opens the windows of heaven to bless His faithful children (Malachi 3:10): God says, *"Test me!"* He wants to be tested. He does not say pray for the harvest; He says pray for the laborers! Basically the principle is that *"A man reaps whatever he sows"* (Galatians 6:7).

When believers are obedient to God's principles, He says that He will stop the enemy from destroying the blessings (Malachi 3:11). Satan's job is to destroy everything believers do that is godly and scriptural. Satan's ministry is stealing, killing, and mass destruction. Believers need the protection of God in their finances to cover their labor. God's principles working in the lives of believers are the only refuge. When a believer does not live by biblical financial principles, he gives Satan access to his harvest. The irony of spiritual principles is that any giver prospers. Proverbs 11:25 states: *"A generous man will prosper; he who refreshes others will himself be refreshed."*

This is not contingent on the believer's religious or spiritual state. The difference between Christian giving and other forms of giving is that Christians sow to the Spirit (of God) whereas others sow only to the flesh (sinful nature).

Believers must pray not only that the strongholds are pulled down and destroyed but that the effects of their assignment and all evidence of their presence be gone as well.

Signs, Symptoms, and Manifestations of the Spirit of Poverty, Financial Curses and Lack:

Non-Tithing	Living Above Means	Famine
Judgment	Hoarding	Stinginess
Ignorance	Pestilence	Deprivation
Ignorance	Sickness	Fraud
Pauperism	Embezzlement	Inability to Make or Keep Money
Begrudging	Giving	Greed
Oppression	Defraud	Gambling
Drug-Trafficking	Destitution	Financial Curse
Shortage	Hardship	Pride
Waste	Extravagance	Indigence
Debt	Fear of Lack	Selfishness
Ingratitude	Depression	Want
Addiction	Shame	Laziness

Pray for the release of: prosperity, liberality in giving, faith, truth, and abundance.

Deliverance: In Physical Health Areas

Deliverance and healing are under the awesome power of the Lord Jesus Christ, yesterday, today, and forever (Hebrew 13:8). God has not changed and is able to meet the needs of the body, soul, and spirit of man. The Bible states that being in good health is important in 3 John 2: *"Beloved, I wish above all things that thou mayest prosper and be in health, even as thy soul prospereth."* God is concerned about the believer's body and soul; to neglect the physical health of the body or indulge in the body's sinful desires is not being in alignment with the discipline that keeps us in the best condition to serve in the kingdom of God. In Matthew 15:26, Jesus calls healing and deliverance of the Canaanite woman's daughter, *"The children's bread."* Healing and deliverance are gifts from God intended for His children. Sickness is the result of sin, and the presence of sin in the world is a direct indication of the influence and power of Satan. The Bible says death entered the world through sin.

> *"Wherefore, as by one man sin entered into the world, and death by sin; and so death passed upon all men, for that all have sinned." (Romans 5:12)*

Jesus came to redeem (rescue and deliver) sinners from sin and death. Sickness is a result of sin, and death is the completed state of sickness that has matured. Christians must view life through the lens of scriptural truth rather than that of experience. The scripture teaches that supernatural forces are continually at work in this world. The Gospels record that many of the healings were actually deliverances. In a broad sense and by practical definition, being delivered is to be healed, and healing is deliverance. 1 Corinthians 6:15 states: *"Know ye not that your bodies are the members of Christ?"* This truth cannot be altered and yet remain true, for the altered truth becomes a lie. The gospel of Jesus Christ was true then and is true today. Luke 9:11 (compare with Matthew 12:15; Acts 10:38) says, *"He healed all that came unto Him."*

Thus, coming to Jesus qualifies one to be healed and the standard is thus set in the scriptures. The scripture does not say that Jesus healed only the faithful, the rich, or the poor; it says that He healed "all that came to Him." Further, 1 John 3:8 also says, *"For this cause was the Son of God manifested that He might destroy the works of the devil."* The works of the devil are clearly visible today, manifested in sicknesses and afflictions that are sometimes the result of specific sins. Jesus commanded the man at the Pool of Bethesda, *"Sin no more, lest a worse thing come upon thee"* (John 5:14).

This man was lame and suddenly able to walk, but not without a warning. Jesus admonished the man to *sin no more*. Sin is the reason sickness has come into the world. Had there been no sin in the world (beginning at the Fall recorded in Genesis 3), there would have been no sickness or disease. In another instance, the disciples asked:

> *"Master, who did sin, this man or his parents, that he was born blind? Jesus quickly corrected them saying, "Neither this man nor his parents sinned said Jesus, but this happened so that the work of God might be manifested in his life." (John 9:2)*

God does at times, as in this case, allow sickness or suffering so that faith in God is increased and God is thereby glorified. Not all sickness is a result of specific sins, individually committed, yet the spiritual principle is that sin in the broad sense is ultimately the cause of sickness. Sin, sickness, and death are the triple curses of the devil. Jesus did not heal the sick for them to become Christians; rather, He healed them because it was His nature to heal, to deliver, to set free the captives. In Luke 6:19, we read that *"There went virtue out of Him [Jesus] and healed them all."*

God's virtue is His goodness.

In dealing with sickness many times Jesus rebuked it, using the same method as with demons. This shows that He considered sickness as the work of a demon. Luke 4:35 states:

> *"And Jesus rebuked him…And when the devil had thrown him in the midst, he came out of him and hurt him not."*

Another example is in the case of Jesus' healing of Peter's mother-in-law: *"And he stood over her, and rebuked the fever; and it left her" (Luke 4:39).*

Afflictions are the physical or mental conditions of the body, soul, or spirit. The medical community today is coming to the realization that anger, stress, hatred, fear, and guilt are responsible for many organic diseases such as cancers, diseases of the reproductive system, the nervous system, stomach ulcers, arthritis, heart trouble, digestive system diseases, etc. These organ systems can directly as well as indirectly become entry points for demonic influence. Many people have no real understanding about how God desires man to function in a healthy harmony as body, soul, and spirit. Many people with afflictions are oblivious to the fact that their bodily symptoms could quite possibly stem from an emotional issue or trauma, which resonated from an unfavorable childhood experience. It is possible to be afflicted with sickness in any or all of our created being—body, soul, or spirit—because of the presence of an evil spirit or demon that is operating in some area of our lives.

Physical illness and sickness of the body, however, is much easily identifiable. Therefore, when a part of the body is damaged or not functioning properly, people typically settle for a diagnosis of being ill and even accept a prognosis of illness unto death. The body is the temple of the Holy Spirit and is related to social morality, spiritual morality, diet, and exercise. Any misuse of the temple is contrary to being good stewards over the physical image God has given us.

Deliverance: In Emotional/ Psychological Areas

Human emotions are a gift from the Creator, God has given mankind the inner ability to love and enjoy pleasure. They are created with the capacity to want and feel in their emotions and because of that they value pleasure. It is normal to love pleasure; however, it is that part of mankind that competes with the Lord for his heart. Believers need to discipline their lives to love godly pleasures and receive fulfillment from the work of Christ in their lives. The love of pleasure renders the emotions very powerful within the thinking processes. They have the ability to drive man's thinking according to his wants, desires, feelings, or inclinations to self-gratification. Emotions hold the power. Emotions are an expression of the inner feelings and should be governed by a renewed mind in Christ (Romans 12:1-2).

If personal fulfillment apart from Christ is one's goal, then he is headed in the wrong direction and will be open to the counsel of his emotions rather than the Word of God. People commonly seek self-satisfaction and gratification by doing what they think they need to do, based on their fleshly emotions, which promise fulfillment. In the end, they fade into vain hope and the temporal joy they provide can be removed in an instant. Because nothing is consistent in this world, at any time things are subject to change; only a heart anchored in and under the control of Christ can find true joy, peace, contentment, and lasting fulfillment. The flesh can never be satisfied, and the end result is emotional suffering and a life without joy and peace.

The problem with emotions is they have the power to rule choices and behavior, which means if a believer looks to people or things for pleasure and fulfillment, then he has not made a decision to love God first.

Emotions are extremely deceptive, and an emotionally-healthy person is one who has learned to renew his mind and emotions by the Word of God. If one never learns to exercise control over his emotions, then he give the powers of darkness an emotional foothold, which will only lead to a more aggressive demonic influence. In order to be emotionally and spiritually healthy, one has to be in control of his thoughts and feelings. Wounded emotions tend to be irresponsible in that they become unruly, disobedient, lie, cheat, and demand their own way.

Problems will not disappear overnight, but believers have a choice not to let Satan rob them of their freedom to choose. The choice is the ability to say "yes" or "no" to sin, but the Bible says we are to be *dead to sin*. This does not mean believers must *feel* dead to sin. In many instances, in fact, believers may feel very alive to it, but the truth is based on what the Word of God says—not on *feelings*.

Romans 6:1,2,6,7 (KJV) states:

> "*What shall we say then? Shall we continue in sin,*
> *that grace may abound? God forbid. How shall we,*

that are dead to sin, live any longer therein? Know-
ing this, that our old man is crucified with Him, that
the body of sin might be destroyed, that henceforth
we should not serve sin. For he that is dead is freed
from sin…. Because I am free, I can count myself
dead to sin and alive to God."

The answer to emotional health and well-being is freedom, being delivered and set free by the power of God. Freedom gives believers the assurance that their need for security, significance, love, and acceptance are always met in Christ. Free people do not have to push themselves to be the greatest, the best, or to fix every problem. Deliverance and freedom are the result of resting in Christ. This assurance cannot be shaken by circumstances or personal bondages. When people are delivered emotionally and set free, they realize that identity does not depend on performance. Experiencing freedom is totally believing God and acting on the basis of the truth regardless of feelings.

Everyone has areas of his life that are out of control, whether it is in health, finances, marriages, children, etc. The drive for control in these areas of life keeps one from resting in Jesus Christ. Once the truth is realized, the person comes to the conclusion that he is not in control of the matters of life and has no ability to control these areas. This is God's job description. Though the believer may have input in this or that matter, the good news is that God is in control.

Emotional / Psychological Signs, Symptoms, Conditions

- **Schizophrenia**—*"an emotional illness greatly affected by interpersonal deviance"* (Beck & Demarest, 2005). Schizophrenia is a mental disease marked by a breakdown in the relation between thoughts, feelings, and actions frequently accompanied by delusions and retreat from social life. In the case of demonic activity, the schizophrenic's personality (the real personality) has never developed, owing to demonic interference. The demonic personalities of rejection (inward) and rebellion (outward) have taken over, causing a split personality or a rupture in the psyche.

- **Loneliness**—isolation, alienation, withdrawal.

- **Restlessness**—insomnia, roving, nervousness, worry, anxiety, tension, impatience.

- **Suicide**—self-destruction, depression, gloominess, discouragement, death, despair, hopelessness, death wish, insanity, madness, confusion, rejection.

- **Superstition**—spirits operating under witchcraft, delusion, deception, fear, accidents, demons, ghosts, idolatry.

- **Sorcery**—drugs (Greek: *pharmakeia*), witchcraft, magic, occult, charms, incantation, hypnotism, trance, spells.

- **Spiritism**—séance, spirit guide, necromancy.

- **Rejection**—spirits operating under **rebellion** include accusation, selfishness, pride, hatred, resentment, violence, disobedience, suspicion, stubbornness, anger, unteachableness; rejection from mother, father, siblings; self-rejection; rejection from the womb; hurt, deep hurt, wounded, bruised, low self-esteem. These can open the door for spirits or rebellion, pride, bitterness, escape, guilt, inferiority, disrespect, hardness, unworthiness, intolerance, timidity, and shyness.

- **Retaliation**—spirits operating under revenge, spite, bitterness, murder, self-vindication, eye for an eye, counterattack, reprisal, malice, rage.

- **Developmental Disability**—impediment, handicap, hindrance, obstruction.

- **Rebellion**—spirits operating under rebellion include accusation, selfishness, pride, hatred violence, persecution, bitterness, witchcraft.

- **Strife**—spirits operating under contention, arguing, fighting, confusion envy (James 3:16), discord, competition, anger, hatred, rage.

- **Suspicion**—distrust, fear, paranoia, doubt, rejection, hurt, accusation.

- **Nervousness**—spirit operating under fear, tension, anxiety, apprehension, restlessness, worry, timidity.

- **Mental Illness**—operating under insanity, madness, mania, senility paranoia, hallucinations, schizophrenia, developmental or cognitive disability.

- **Madness**—insanity, mania, mental illness, neurosis, caused by oppression (Ecclesiastes 7:7), by idolatry (Jeremiah 50:38), and by a curse (Deuteronomy 28:28).

- **Escape**—withdrawal, passivity, sleepiness, stoicism, alcohol, drugs, silence, depression, apathy.

- **Fear**—of decisions, being hurt, the future, crowds, being wrong; horror, panic, fright, sudden fear, terror, dread, apprehension; causes torment (1 John 4:18).

- **Cursing**—blasphemy, coarse jesting, gossip, criticism, profanity, abuse, swearing, bitterness, belittling, railing.

CHAPTER 6

Exposing Demonic Entry Points

K NOWING HOW demons enter a person is in most cases essential to understanding how they will leave. A demon can enter a person only if it has legal rights to do so. Removing the legal rights is crucial for effective Deliverance Ministry. The process of removing the rights of demons is in many instances a matter of first identifying and exposing the entry points. Exposing demonic entry points is paramount because of the crafty devices used. Sins of the flesh are always doorways to the demonic realm. However, demons, evil spirits, dominions and powers come into direct and indirect contact with the people of God. This happens because Christians live in the world and are products of the environment.

The modern conveniences and access to information is passed through the televisions, computers, the Internet, telephones, etc., providing opportunities for the transmission of both good and corrupt information. A person can knowingly and unknowingly establish entry points in their lives, homes, marriages, families, churches, work, and nations. Through these various common daily living and working devices and practices, demons can contact people and open them up to the perverse reality of the spirit world. The demon world has established many entrapments and avenues of destruction through which to establish entry points. Territory given to demons legally through entry points must be reclaimed. If legal rights are not removed, demons cannot be successfully cast out.

Many times people want to be free from the torment and pain inflicted by demons when they are yet to make Jesus Christ Lord of their lives. One of the most serious conditions that invites demonic influence in the Body of Christ is a shallow relationship with Jesus Christ. A relationship that has not been consummated and grounded in love for the Lord can never touch the depth of the soul. This exposes one to the enemy's attacks and operates as an entry point for the demonic. Many satanic attacks come when a person assumes that abstinence is a means of deliverance. Abstinence is a discipline that in some instances produces temporary positive results. To cease from indulgence or withholding oneself from participating in an act can be achieved by believers as well as unbelievers, but it is not deliverance. Deliverance must be a sincere salvation experience of being rescued from a situation from which one was powerless to deliver himself. It is accompanied by the experience of true freedom coupled with dedication and a willingness to be set free. Deliverance is more than abstinence. The objective is a permanent state. Ephesians 4:27 admonishes: "Neither give place to the devil."

Entry Through Sin

The Tyndale Bible Dictionary defines sin as "Evildoing that is not only against humanity, society, others, or oneself, but against God. Sin is transgressing, violating, or trespassing God's laws in the Bible." Sin occurs when one operates outside of God's prescription for life. God sets the ideal or the standard for human behavior. The biblical words for sin speak of violating or transgressing that standard in some way (Greek hamartia is a term from the sport of archery that denotes "missing the target"). Whether sin is committed knowingly or unknowingly, the consequences are the same. Satan's entry into one's life implies influence from an external demonic attack and not demonic possession. Demonic possession implies possession of one's faculties. Satan operates within boundaries that God has established as spiritual laws. Outside of these boundaries he has no authority or power to enforce his plans. This is why Satan uses traps to bring people into his boundaries so he can attack them. He attacks to gain legal access, which may be spiritual, social, material, and/or physical.

In Romans 6:7,11,12,13, Paul issues a warning to believers:

"For he that is dead is freed from sin…. Because I am free, I can count myself dead to sin and alive to God. Likewise reckon ye also yourselves to be dead indeed unto sin, but alive unto God through Jesus Christ our Lord….When we choose not to let sin rule in our members and not obey its desires. Let not sin therefore reign in your mortal body, that ye should obey it in the lusts thereof. Neither yield ye your members as instruments of unrighteousness unto sin: but yield yourselves unto God as those that are alive from the dead, and your members as instruments of righteousness unto God."

Throughout the scriptures, we see that God has purposed to deal with sin once and forever, judging sin by way of the cross and thus making possible the annihilation of sin forever. Since the old creation has been contaminated by sin, God is going to provide a new creation in which sin will never be an issue again. Human beings are caught in the midst of this conflict of the ages and are part of God's plan to deal with sin and all the evil forces.

There are major avenues for demonization, which are identifiable sin areas that bring about demonization or demonic influences. These sin areas do not automatically lead to demonization, and where it does occur it can range from mild to severe. Deliverance also can vary from instantaneous to cases where the victim may need to practice self-deliverance (spiritual warfare focused on breaking the demonic strongholds within one's own life) over a period of time or seek the help of others for full deliverance (Murphy, 2006).

Generational Sin

Generational sin is judgment that moves through a family line. It begins before infancy and continues through adulthood. In many cases, demons are identified with a family line. It is sometimes called transference, inheritance, or familiar spirits. Jeremiah 32:18 states:

> *"Thou showest lovingkindness unto thousands, and recompensest the iniquity of the fathers into the bosom of their children after them: the Great, the Mighty God, the Lord of hosts, is his name."*

Numbers 14:18 states:

> *"The Lord is slow to anger and abundant in lovingkindness, forgiving iniquity and transgression; but He will by no means clear the guilty, visiting the iniquity of the fathers on the children to the third and the fourth generations."*

Biblically speaking, there is no teaching or example of demonic transference in the scriptures. There are warnings that the sins of parents can have devastating consequences on their children. In Exodus 20:5-6, Deuteronomy 5:9-10, 18:9-14, these warnings are given in the context of heads of families, usually males, who have rebelled against God and are involved in serving other gods. God says of such men: "They hate Him" (Exodus 20:5).

Child Abuse

The victim of child abuse becomes the victim of the sin of others, usually trusted authority figures in their childhood or youth. Children are the most vulnerable and defenseless of all human beings. They cannot protect themselves from human and supernatural evil. Adults are their primary protectors. As a result, children are susceptible to demonization. Children become adults, parents, and grandparents. Damaged, demonized adults tend to raise damaged, demonized children and grandchildren. The most strategic way to destroy humanity is to destroy the children. The greatest good to do to humanity is to protect and heal its damaged children.

Four Interrelated Classifications of Child Abuse	
Type of Abuse	**Negative Reactions**
Sexual Abuse	Extreme shame and sexual problems. Fear and anger.
Physical Abuse	Extreme rage and interpersonal relationship problems.
Psychological Abuse	Extreme negative self-image and spirit of rejection.
Religious Abuse	Extreme confusion about God and the Christian faith.

The worst possible type of child abuse occurring today is Satanic Ritual Abuse (SRA). SRA is a combination of all four forms of abuse. It is religious abuse performed on a child that causes unspeakable pain. It is physical abuse related to sexual abuse, often rape and perversion of every imaginable (and unimaginable)

type. It results in the most extreme form of psychological damage. The child is preprogrammed in this ultimate evil to function
as a youth and as an adult. Often the abuse splits the personality
of the child, producing personality disassociation leading to Multiple Personality Disorder (MPD). Research reveals that 75% or
more of MPDs resulted from SRA and related forms of extreme
child sexual abuse (Ross, 1995).

Anger, Bitterness, Rage, Rejection, and Rebellion

These sins usually result from wrong or alleged wrong done in
childhood or youth and continue into adulthood. Most demons
of anger, bitterness, rage, rejection, and rebellion come after the
abuse as reactionary sin and can open the door to demons, as the
victim gives way to anger and rage over what has happened.
Many demonic problems experienced by believers are associated
with broken family relationships and a destructive ("demon-
friendly") family environment. Child abuse and dysfunctional
home life are the most common causes of demons' attaching to
the life of children.

Sexual Sins

Sexual sins and sexual malfunctions of all types are a common
entry point or door to demonic involvement in the life of believers. In most cases of severe demonization of adult Christians, sexual demons are present. Here are a few suggestions as to why:

1. **Sexuality occupies an important place in human life, for
   it reflects the image of God in man in a unique manner.**
   God as a perfect being possesses all the sublime qualities of
   maleness and femaleness in His one person. While God is
   not sexual, He has created the unique qualities of maleness and femaleness. Thus, neither man nor woman is
   fully complete without the other. Disturbing human sexu-

ality disturbs the whole person. Demons recognize this fact and exploit it for evil.

2. **When people are crippled sexually, their entire being is damaged.** More harm can be done to humanity by debasing sexuality than by almost any other single factor except for spirituality. Thus, the most destructive form of child abuse is not physical abuse but sexual physical abuse. If a religious dimension is added (as in SRA, Satanic Ritual Abuse), the sexual abuse is even more destructive.

3. **Sex is one of the most powerful drives in life.** Men and women face some of their fiercest struggles at this point. Sex out of control leads to some of the greatest personal and social problems faced by humanity. AIDS and abortion result primarily from the abuse of sexuality, as do prostitution, rape, incest, homosexuality, and the unimaginable range of sexual perversions humanity practices.

4. **Demons of sexual abuse and perversion are floating in the air, so to speak everywhere.** They are among the most active, subtle, and vicious of all demons.

Curses

In the Western world, the mindset is that a curse is an expression of anger or displeasure that has no power to inflict evil. However, the Bible opens and closes with curses. God pronounces the first series of curses on Satan, mankind, and the land (Genesis 3:14-19). The last reference to the curse ends in Revelation 22:3:

> *"For man there is no escape from the power of the curse and curses until the new heavens and new earth have come and the saints are glorified with our Lord."*

Curses come from God, God's servants, the spirit world, and Satan's human servants. All four release spiritual energy towards the person or object cursed. Cursing in the Old Testament is a power concept meant to release negative spiritual power against the object, person, or place being cursed. A curse uttered or written in the name of God through His authority figures was considered effective in bringing the judgment of God on the accursed person, place, or thing.

Occult Practices

Believers are at war with two broad types of occultism: non-Christian occultism and Christian occultism.

Non-Christian occultism involves:

1. The horoscope and other astrological practices.
2. The use of Ouija boards and similar methods of direct contact with the power of the spirit world.
3. Fantasy role-playing games involving the spirit world (a popular example is "Dungeons and Dragons").
4. The acceptance and use of any psychic powers from pre-conversion days.
5. All attempts to seek psychic or spiritual healings.
6. Any practice of ESP, clairvoyance, levitation, telekinesis, astral projection, automatic handwriting, and similar practices. Most of these induce the operation of evil spirits.
7. Any involvement in the cults, séances, belief in reincarnation, attempts to contact the dead.
8. All Eastern and mystic religions and other non-Christian religions.

Christian occult activity involves:

Seeking for or accepting spiritual experiences within a "Christian" context without examining their true source and the motives for seeking such experiences from the perspective of the truth of God's Word, scripture (1 John 4:1).

Demonic Entry through Deliberate and Non-Deliberate Curses

Curses from men fall into two categories (Horrobin, 2003). (1) Deliberate curses applied by those who are working within the occult and know exactly what they are doing and, whether they appreciate it or not, are using demons to invoke harm on the victim of the curse. (2) Non-deliberate curses that, though they are not be cast deliberately, are curses nonetheless because they fall into the general category of words spoken against another person that are contrary to God's plan and purposes for that person.

Deliberate Curses

We can learn from the ways those who deliberately place curses operate. They cannot just choose someone at random and speak a curse against him. In order to be effective, they have to have some form of link with the person that can be used as an access point to the victim. It is as if the demons that will fulfill the curse have to have knowledge of the victim or a means of identifying him. This explains why something that belongs to the person is used in cursing rituals. An object the victim owns is frequently used, such as an item of clothing or a piece of jewelry. When an object or a piece of clothing is stolen, for example, it can be used in an attempt to curse its owner. Alternatively, a curse (demon) can be attached to the object and then returned to the owner so that the demon or curse is able to operate directly against the victim.

Something of the person's flesh is especially powerful. Nail clippings, hair trimmings, and blood are frequently used. The scripture talks about "the life of the soul as being in the blood," and the use of someone's blood in the cursing ritual as a means of linking a curse directly to the victim seems to be one of the most powerful means of controlling people through demonic cursing.

Another method of linking the curse to the victim is the use of his photograph. This is more commonly a voodoo practice, in which the photograph is used instead of a voodoo doll to inflict physical pain and symptoms on the victim. For example, by stabbing the doll or the photograph in a specific place, the voodooist can use demons to induce commensurate symptoms in the body of the victim.

Non-deliberate Curses

Non-deliberate curses are curses spoken by people against others but not with the specific intention of bringing harm to the person in the sense described in the previous section. Ignorance of how the demonic appropriates the things believers say and do does not prevent the demons from using those words and deeds to hurt others.

For example, the enemy can latch on to what we say in a fit of anger and make it stick in the mind or the emotions of the person to whom they were spoken. If the words are believed and accepted, the demonic can then establish itself, holding the victim to the words that have been said. For this to happen there has to be some connection between the one who curses and the victim. More often than not, the people who say things to each other that really hurt already have a soul tie (marital conflict, disputes with friends, parent-child conflict). It is by virtue of the fact that the people share an emotional bond that the words have such devastating power to curse. Negative and destructive words exchanged between emotionally-bound people become a landing ground for the demonic.

For deliverance and healing to occur, believers must recognize, repent, and renounce all curses, generational bondages, and ungodly soul-ties.

Demonic Entry Through Addictions

Addiction is a manifestation of the spirit of bondage. Anything that binds one in such a way that he or she becomes an involuntary slave falls under the category of a spirit of bondage. To experience the freedom of God only to return to Satan's bondage happens. One of the hallmarks of demonic activity is being out of control. The act of control is integral to the nature of addictions. Once a person is out of control in his behavior because of his choices, clearly addiction has set in and control is not in his hands. The pertinent question for Deliverance Ministry is: Whose hands is control now in—once the person has "lost control"?

What is addiction?

What is the unseen force that causes people to abuse substances that in the beginning produce mentally enticing and physically stimulating effects and cause people to act contrary to their moral and logical reasoning but in the end bring bondage even unto death? Addiction creates an insane mindset and causes people to become powerless and enslaved to its effects to the point of denial of the power. The power of the addiction leads to a bondage that in time becomes physically and mentally unmanageable. It has the ability to consume the very life and spirit of man.

Let's look at two probable aspects of addiction on a higher level-addiction as spiritual and addiction as physical.

- **If Addiction is Spiritual:** The means of acquiring the problem of addiction is a result of a spiritual force. Thus, resolving the problem must be spiritual and must be dealt with from the realm from which it originated—the spirit realm. There is no way to fight a spiritual battle by merely physical, material means. Therefore, there is no effective means of defense in our flesh or physical bodies to engage in a fight in the spiritual realm and no knowledge of the source of the problem. It is hard to fight an "unknown" enemy.

- **If Addiction is Physical:** The battle-plan would be to identify the source of the problem, then use the appropriate weapons and fight. The battlefield then becomes equal. We are material beings. The issues and the substance are surely a reality within our means and grasp. Thus, we simply assume control of the situation, set the time, pick the place, and wage war against it and proceed to fight, or better yet: Just say no.

But a more holistic approach to addiction is to consider it both spiritual and physical. Perhaps two entities, sometimes working together and sometimes working independently, under either a positive or a negative influence or power. Positive is (God or good). Negative is (Satan or evil).

The web of bondage does not happen in a day. Rather it is a process that develops gradually over time. A person will engage in a series of steps designed to satisfy the desires of the flesh before suddenly realizing that he is in a trap again, and it is too late simply to stop the thought or behavior. The spirit of addiction is a very complex illness and can manifest in different ways, with physical and psychological symptoms and wide-scale social ramifications.

Often enough, there is a generational spirit of addiction that needs to be addressed. It is essential in the process of deliverance from the spirit of addiction to renounce the demonic assignment over the family line and forbid the spirit from going continuing on to the children. Of course, the underlying needs of an addict must be carefully evaluated in order to bring full healing. But if the demonic dimension is ignored in the healing process, it is almost impossible for one to come through an addictive problem and remain clean and free. Addiction and all of its sequels affects not only the addict but his family, friends, and social environment. Naturally speaking, the way to recovery is long and painful, and there is always the danger of relapse.

One of the hallmarks of demonic activity is behavior that is out of control. This is especially true with regard to addictions. A sign of drug addiction is when one is unable to control his behavior through free-will choice and is, instead, controlled by chemically-addictive substances or behaviors.

Freedom from addiction requires:

- Confession and repentance for mistreating the body.
- Exercising the will in wanting to be healed and delivered.
- Wanting deliverance from any demon that has gained access through the addiction.
- A disciplined lifestyle.

For many who are addicted, the root cause is much deeper than the addiction. Their addictive behavior is usually a compensating factor for a greater problem. Many times, the addictive behavior is a cry for help. Addictions begin as "treatment" or "cure" for a symptom: The person is using the substance or engaging in the addictive behavior as a way to kill emotional pain or escape from reality. In some cases, the drug is a "friend" for the lonely or an anesthetic for numbing guilt. Popular conceptions of addiction have expanded to include gambling, eating, chocolate, playing computer games, using the Internet, even such healthful behaviors as exercise when taken to extremes. Non-substance-related addictive behaviors are similar to any drug addiction in that the person has a lack of control over his actions and behaviors.

The enemy is sophisticated in keeping people in bondage. As humanity progresses, Satan continues to reinvent himself and forge new weapons of mass destruction (Anderson & Quarles, 1996). There are popular and professional definitions of what an addiction is. In everyday language, we think of someone who is addicted as having what we call an "unhealthy habit." Those who are mature in the Lord, however, know that behind these so-called addictions are demonic spirits.

Addiction Defined

1. The progressive abuse of substance or behavior that is repetitious and difficult or impossible to control;
2. The engagement in a compulsive behavior (in some cases compulsions and obsessions).

Basically, an addiction is something that a person enjoys doing, or at least started off enjoying, and involves some degree of physical dependence. An obsession, on the other hand, is an idea or a thought that dominates a person's mind. A compulsion is an irresistible urge or a repetitive behavior. A related complex that involves addictions, obsessions, and compulsions is obsessive-compulsive disorder (OCD).

Categories of Addiction

- **Substance:** alcohol, heroin, tobacco, solvents, cocaine, cannabis, caffeine, methadone, benzodiazepines, hallucinogens, amphetamines, ecstasy, painkillers, barbiturates, steroids.
- **Social:** exercise, sex, sexual perversion, pornography, eating (anorexia, bulimia, etc.), television, techno (computer games; cyber-sex, etc.), work, gambling, rock music, people.

Regardless of why people choose to drink or take drugs, each person with an addiction has at least two of the following three conditions (Twerski, 1997):

1. Their basic needs are not being met in appropriate or legitimate ways.
2. They have not learned how to cope with life's problems.
3. They cannot seem to resolve their personal or spiritual conflicts in responsible ways.

The chemicals they become addicted to will not meet their needs nor enable them to cope with life nor resolve their spiritual conflicts in responsible ways. The addiction will only make matters worse. It is important to remember that nobody plans to become addicted and nobody enjoys addiction.

Alcoholism

Alcoholic beverage are one of the most prominent and popular legal substances, with near universal social acceptance in our society. When a person becomes addicted to alcohol, however, it is considered a disease by members of the medical profession, as is drug abuse. Many in pulpit and pew alike indulge in alcohol and drug use. This is a serious social issue and the Church would do well to recognize that those in the Church are susceptible to the world and its ways. Being a Christian does not render one immune to addiction. 1 Thessalonians 5:7, 8 states:

> "For those who sleep do their sleeping at night and those who get drunk get drunk at night. But since we are of the day, let us be sober, having put on the breastplate of faith and love, and as a helmet, the hope of salvation."

Though alcoholics have all kinds of excuses as to why they use alcohol, they all have one thing in common—the illusion of being in control. Most of the people addicted to alcohol or drugs lose control over the chemical; yet they continue to believe they can control it. Even in the face of overwhelming evidence that their lives have become totally unmanageable, they still insist that they are in charge. The reality behind this denial is that they cannot bear to admit they have lost control. Addicts who think they have control over a chemical or drug are delusional and possess a false sense of power brought on by the substance. This is addictive thinking and a delusion of power and must be overcome before the admission of powerlessness can be accepted.

The key to overcoming denial is recognizing that there are many things in life that man has no control over, such as the weather, other people, time, physical aspects of the body, and psychological functions. As the alcoholic or addict surrenders the delusion of power—the hallmark of addictive thinking—he is able to admit that there is a higher power—God. At that point the person must lose faith in his own reasoning and learn that his concept of reality and thought processes are distorted. This is the point at which ministering can be received, and the Deliverance Minister can introduce the addict to the possibility of another version of reality—Truth.

Most alcoholics learn through experience that alcohol produces a sense of gratification. In the natural realm, the person is seeking to quench an insatiable emptiness that exists in the spirit of man. Substances may give temporary gratification, but the problem still remains and in most cases has never been challenged. It is easy to identify and satisfy the symptoms of hunger, cold, thirst, loneliness, or other physical needs, but it is hard to know what it takes to satisfy hunger in the spirit. The spirit of man is the part that separates man from animals and gives him a degree of intelligence that allows him to be morally free. This spirit of man comes with the knowledge of, and capacity to, deny ourselves behaviors that our body lusts for. These are unique to mankind and constitute the spirit of man, which also has the capacity to choose whether to recognize their spirituality and their relationship with God.

The Cycle of Addiction

"The first step to addiction is habit."

The first drink, puff, or snort causes an immediate onset of chemical reaction in the body and the person feels a "rush." The baseline experience is different for those searching for a temporary reprieve from the pressures of life. Active addicts repeat their actions even though they know that they are destructive. Their purpose in life has become getting high. They cannot delay gratification and do not consider the consequences of their actions. They are usually a bundle of nerves or depressed. They are looking for something to lift their spirits or calm their nerves. Drugging tends to help them mellow out. And the devil of it is that it works! Unfortunately, the effects wear off. Each person travels down a private path to addiction, but the downward spiraling cycles are all similar, and in the end the addict lacks freedom. He is unfortunately dominated by the compulsion of addiction.

The first step to recovery is to admit one has a problem. How do people recover from the cycle of addiction? First of all, they must realize and come to terms with the fact that the problem is not alcohol or drugs; the problem is coping with life and its problems and storms. Their problems are physical, mental, emotional, and spiritual. The spiritual is often overlooked in secular treatment programs. Yet it is the most important factor in treatment. Everyone born in this world is physically alive and spiritually dead (Ephesians 2:1). All alike are hopeless without God. No one living independently from God can live a holy life. Fear of being exposed drives people away from the light that reveals their sin. God's unconditional love and acceptance is the only remedy for this hideous condition. Truth is the answer. Facing the truth is the one thing that everyone who is seeking deliverance from bondage must do. What they need to come out of is the lie that the enemy has led them to believe. Secret sin is Satan's breeding ground; shame is an issue as well.

This is why living a lie is more devastating than facing the shame of being exposed. Sobriety is not the answer; it deals with only a small part of reality. People need to be taught that their deliverance is in Christ, and they need to be shown how Christ can meet their critical and personal needs. Programs don't save people, nor can they set people free. Only Jesus can do that. Isaiah 5:11 states:

> *"Woe to those who rise early in the morning that they may pursue strong drink; Who stay up late in the evening that wine may inflame them!"*

The Lord loves humans too much to let them walk in darkness and live a lie. When they live a lie they play right into Satan's hands, for he is the father of lies. This is why in the early stages of life Satan makes it easy for people to learn to live independent of God. Then the day a person decides to give his life to Christ, he is a new creation in Christ. However, everything in his memory is still there. Nobody pushed a button and cleared the memory.

This is why Paul says in Romans 12:2:

"Do not conform to this world, but be ye trans-formed by the renewing of your mind, then you will prove what is God's good and perfect will."

The primary programming of minds takes place early in childhood. Children are naturally open and inquisitive and thus very vulnerable to spirits, positive as well as negative. The mind is where strongholds are first established.

- First, strongholds can arise through experiences and environments, such as the family in which the child is raised, parents' childrearing practices, the church/es the child does or does not attend, the neighborhoods and communities in which they live, the friends they have. Every experience has an effect on the developing mind and the person's view of the world. The environment, however, is not the only thing that determines how the person develops.

- Second, strongholds can arise through traumatic experiences such as abuse (physical, emotional, psychological), neglect, rape, parental conflict, separation, or divorce, absence of parent/s, death of loved ones. All these are intense experiences that can cause serious trauma to the mind of a child. These experiences carry over into adulthood and can lead to struggles with the daily issues of life.

Because man is in this world he is continually tempted. Satan knows exactly what his appetites, wants, and weaknesses are and just what it takes to entice him to satisfy those fleshly desires. Thus, Christians must know the truth about temptation and understand that being tempted is not in and of itself a sin. Hebrews 4:15 states, "Jesus was tempted in every way, yet was without sin."

Every temptation of the enemy is intended to get one to live outside of the will of God. Satan has been tempting man from the beginning; therefore, it is not strange to believers because every temptation begins with a thought in the mind. The challenge is to learn how to stand in the midst of constant temptation. Demons have the ability to influence through any medium that has access to the thoughts and emotions. Anything that a person finds appealing has the potential to open his heart to the wiles of the devil.

This is why television and movies are dangerous. What is seen with the eyes has a powerful effect on the emotions. Visual stimulation opens the door of the heart and makes one vulnerable to temptation. Emotions search for pleasure, and if one is willing to find pleasure in sin then pleasure will become a source of spiritual bondage. Believers will be affected spiritually by the pleasures they allow themselves to experience. From early childhood through adulthood, people's minds are bombarded through the media, advertisements, television, magazines, and movies, as well as with socially acceptable images of euphoria associated with alcohol, drugs, and sex.

The imprint of enticement, once formed, is difficult to disregard or ignore. These are the doors of opportunity for spiritual demonic entrance; this is where strongholds are erected. This is the very reason God has made a "way of escape." The believer has to take the original thought captive to the obedience of Christ and allow the Word of God to define him and begin to exercise God's agenda in his life. It is the Holy Spirit through the Word of God that removes the strongholds in lives and restores the life back to a condition of being Spirit-led. Whatever the cost, believers must be determined to be free in Christ. The victory is in Christ by the blood of Jesus and by the Word of God.

The enemy is a master at keeping people in bondage. He continues to reinvent himself and develop new weapons of destruction for mankind. The Body of Christ must remember that the mind is the seat of all spiritual and carnal thought. Thus, victory is in a renewed mind that has been transformed by the power of God. Believers have the power in the authority of Jesus Christ to deny entrance to their mind by speaking the promises of God to every thought, imagination, and emotion. Authority is the way to the process of deliverance; authority is the right to use power. The Word of God is an effective defense against unclean spirits. Man's deliverance is as close as his mouth. Once a believer understands his authority in Jesus Christ, he can then resist and overcome spiritual attacks when they come. Believers must take personal responsibility for their actions in order to be delivered and set free. Every fiber of a believer's being should have the knowledge that Jesus Christ is greater than Satan, and the blood of Jesus is greater than sin. Deliverance is the assurance that man's need for security, significance, love, acceptance, and worth are all met in Christ.

The Demonic Realm

Symptoms and Manifestations of Demonization

Though demonic possession is a rare event, it is more common than many people realize. The purpose of this section of the study is to inform believers (especially Deliverance Ministers) about demonic possession. It is intended to diagnose anyone. Science is based on verifiable knowledge and, as such, has the potential of changing. What was considered a scientific fact yesterday is still questionable today because further research could bring different findings. Modern science has largely renamed what used to be considered as demonic activity and replaced even the concept of demons with diseases of the mind. Though diseases of the mind are indeed real and medication does improve the quality of life for some, science has not and cannot prove that diabolic infestation does not occur in people. There are many cases where people are emotionally disturbed as a result of mental illness. And there are cases where the person is possessed and also mentally ill. The mental illness may be a result of the possession. There is definitely a thin line between the two.

In his Handbook for Spiritual Warfare, Murphy (2006) writes the following concerning mental illness:

> *"Mental illness is unfortunate. It gives the impression
> that one is crazy, emotionally weak, or too cowardly*

to cope with life. No truly born again believer can become mentally ill, we are often told. He has the mind of Christ so how could his mind become ill? A believer who becomes mentally ill has sin in his life. It is the believer's own fault. If he would only break with the sin patterns in his life, stop worrying trust God, he would become well. Thus, victims of mental illness too often don't find much comfort, sympathy, or help from Christians or churches. Every organ in the believer's body can become diseased or break down, but not his brain or mind. Somehow that cannot happen to a genuine believer."

Sadly, many Christians find the thought of there being a seriously mentally ill Christian repulsive, regardless whether the mental malfunction results from biological-genetic issues, mental/psychological disorders, hormonal imbalances, emotional problems, or social and family system dysfunction. Preachers, communities, families, and churches are a wealth of information on theology and the soul, but psychology refers to the human mind and its function. This is not to disclaim demonic influence in brain malfunction. Wise counseling and experience is a must in these endeavors. It is never wise to diagnose a person's condition beyond the range of your expertise and knowledge. Christian counseling without the gift of discernment and proper training is a dangerous thing. The wise Deliverance Minister will refer a person suspected of having symptoms of mental illness to a well-trained Christian psychiatrist or psychologist.

Demons sometimes enter the body in order to control the individual's thoughts and actions. The symptoms of demonization vary depending on many different factors. One must be cautious not to assume that all cases will manifest the same symptoms. There are three areas of demonic possession. These are mental changes, physical changes, and outward manifestations.

Demonic possession identified by mental changes:

- Changes in personality, usually seen when the victim suddenly becomes very quiet.
- When a usually active person becomes isolated and detached.
- Changes in sleep patterns.
- Significant weight loss or gain not accounted for by dietary changes.
- Behavior becomes hostile.
- Sudden use of profanity that is out of character.
- An aversion to religious talk, church, or objects.
- Self-mutilation.
- Changes in personal hygiene and appearance (fastidious person becomes unkempt).
- May become violent, threatening, and abusive for no reason.
- Blackouts in memory.

All of the above can be psychological, as well as signs of demonic possession. Therefore it is advised to first seek psychological counseling before automatically thinking of possession unless there is clear reasoning for suspect, such as dabbling in the occult, witchcraft or some type of sorcery. Do not mention the possibility of possession to someone that you are suspect of. This could be planting a dangerous seed of emotional distress.

Demonic possession identified by physical changes:

- Staring for long periods of time without blinking the eyes (can indicate a neurological condition as well).
- Person may seem confused (also a sign of mental illness).
- Person speaks a language they couldn't possibly know.
- Speaks in demonic tongues.
- Person becomes completely rigid.
- Eyes change, may turn almost black like a shark.
- Super-human strength.
- The person's voice may fluctuate, from high to low to guttural.
- May be able to tell what you are thinking.
- May seem to glide instead of walk.
- Symbols may appear on the body in the form of welts or scratches (in areas the person cannot reach).
- Levitating.
- Multiple voices coming from the person at the same time.
- Animals appear to be frightened of the person.

Some of these symptoms can be medically related but most of them fall outside of the scientific field. If these signs are observed from this category there is surely cause for concern.

Demonic possession identified by outward manifestations:

- Objects moving around seemingly by themselves.
- Objects disappearing permanently.
- Objects disappear and found in another location.
- Objects seemingly thrown from unseen hands.

- Knocking, banging, or pounding, heard in a room or throughout the house.
- Knocks at the door when no one is there.
- Religious objects disappear or are destroyed.
- Hearing growling.
- Scratching sounds.
- Foul odors, which have no viable source.
- Odd lights.
- Heavy furniture moving on its own.
- Doors and drawers open and close on their own.
- Glass breaks for no reason.
- Physical attacks.
- Psychological attacks.
- Sexual assaults.
- Levitation of objects or people.

There is not always an indication that the person does anything willful or deliberate that would invite demonic activity. The mere absence of the indwelling of the Holy Spirit makes one susceptible to the indwelling of "demonic spirits." When one receives Christ as Lord and Savior, however, he receives a new nature with the capacity for obedience to God and the grace to obey the Word of God through the power of the indwelling Holy Spirit.

Levels of Demonization

There are in fact different levels of demonization; direct demonic contact knowingly or unknowingly can lead to demonic influence for the believer and non-believers and ultimately demonic possession (for the non-believer).

- **The First Level**—Occasional "interaction" with demons via temptation, harassment, and trouble. All believers are involved on a regular basis with demons on this level. This is the starting point to demonic influence, and a person's inclination to a particular sinful disposition. This is the point where Satan projects thoughts and suggestions to a person's mind (no one is exempt).

- **The Second Level**—Regular "participation" with demons "around" the person: Luke 6:18: those who were troubled with unclean spirits.

- **The Third Level**—Painful "affliction" with demons on a person: Luke 13:10-18: the fact that this woman who had a spirit of infirmity for 18 years and is called "a daughter of Abraham" …a covenant child of God.

- **The Fourth Level**—Actual "infestation" with demons in a person (Matthew 9:33-34). Demons cannot live in a Christian unless two conditions exist:

1. They have discovered an entry point.

2. They have a "legal right that allows them to be there (Ephesians 4:27).

- **The Fifth Level**—Total "domination" with demons "in" and "controlling" much of a person's thoughts and actions (Mark 5:1-20). It is most unlikely that a Christian can reach this level of demonization and live.

Seven Steps Satan Uses to Take Over the Soul of a Person

In many cases people who become demon possessed travel down a road influenced by demonic activity. Possession does not occur overnight; time and degenerating actions happen in the life of a person. These steps are reference points not necessarily in this order, and all of these are not taken to reach that point. Christians possess authority from Jesus Christ to cast out evil spirits at any of the steps listed here. There is therefore no reason to fear them.

1. **Regression:** Reversion to earlier behavior patterns: to go backward. To decrease or backslide, to revert to a former level, to reverse a trend, or to shift to a lower state.

   (Revelation 3:16) The opposite of regression is progression, if you are not moving forward, you are probably moving backward. If you are not progressing you are regressing.

   When the devil attacks a human personality, regression is a human battle against his God-given abilities of release and expression. To regress in the human personality is to go backward in spiritual force and power. The human is built for progress, advancement, and understanding. When this is reversed, it is the first warning that negative powers are in play. This can be resisted and overcome by prayer and praise.

2. **Repression:** To restrain: to squeeze; to prevent natural expression; to keep down; to hold back. Repression is the outward sign that regression is taking place on the inside.

   God makes every human an expressionist. The moment a baby is born he begins to express himself. God made man's face to light up and express what is on the inside. Anyone who represses that function is doing the work of the devil. To repress a person is to restrain from without. To repress a personality takes away the joy and gladness of that life. God did not create man to live in a restrained or abnormal environment. Some people have problems with repression because they were raised in a home where they were not allowed to show feelings.

Thus, many times they will wait to see what everyone else thinks before expressing themselves. Repression is something we do to ourselves. Many religions repress the spirit and soul of man and drive back inside the fervent feelings toward God. When the devil destroys a life, one step is the repressing of natural joys.

3. **Suppression:** To press under; to squeeze down abnormally, to keep back; to conceal; to exclude desire and feeling (as to suppress information, feelings, and desires).

   Feelings and desires can be suppressed or kept back. The devil is very keen on suppression. It represents another step toward the beginning of demonic inroads being made into a person's life, the deterioration of emotion and the destruction of full and complete personal happiness. Suppression is an artificial thing imposed from without. It is an unholy action because God and the entire Bible reveal dynamic expression, openness of desire, and exuberant feelings.

   With suppression we have concealment or greater pressures moving against the Christian life. Suppression needs to be broken by the power of God, and cannot be defeated through willpower or by trying harder. It can only be broken by the direct action—taking authority over it in the name of Jesus.

4. **Cognitive or Emotional Disorder:** Depression; a psychotic or neurotic condition characterized by an inability to concentrate; low spirits; gloominess; dejection; sad-

Chapter 7: The Demonic Realm / 135

ness; a decrease in force or activity; an emotional condition with feelings of hopelessness or inadequacy.

In depression there is a "broken spirit." One is pressed down until his spirit is crushed. To remain depressed for a long period of time is of the devil. It is not normal. God does not want anyone depressed or sad. Anyone who stays depressed for an extended time is sick.

The devil takes advantage of people in that lowly state of mind and introduces conflict and confusion that will destroy their happiness, disrupts family and social relationships, and affects one's capacity to work. Depression will destroy every part of a person's natural lives. Many believers are depressed and on various medications for many years. Depression is often triggered by loss, deep troubles, financial burdens, family problems, or disappointments. Depression is dangerous because it brings about an abnormal state of inactivity. The person may sit staring into space, hearing nothing, saying nothing, and doing nothing. Feelings of sadness are also present with feelings too deep to express and too painful to cry. There is a point in depression when apathy reaches the point where one can see no need even to try any longer. There is an example of depression in the book of Psalms:

> *"Why art thou cast down, O my soul? And why art thou disquieted in me? Hope thou in God: for I shall yet praise Him for the help of His countenance." (Psalm 42:5)*

5. **Oppression:** Pressure to crush; to keep one down by severe and unjust use of force or authority; to smother; to overpower or overwhelm; to harass; to ravish; or to rape.

Because of the fear factor in many cases, oppression can be an area far deeper and more involved than depression. The enemy will try to crush the spirit through false guilt of past sins and failures, the attacks of friends and family. Many attacks are through disaster and sorrows and bring an awesome weight of heavy hopelessness and condemnation, leading one to believe that all of one's troubles are due to the judgment and punishment of God. The way out of this kind of attack is to take authority over the power of the enemy—through faith in God's Word, taking dominion over the situation and commanding the Power of God to enter one's life and destroy the works of fear, worry, or nervousness.

6. **Obsession:** To besiege; to haunt as of evil spirits; to be fixed on a single idea to an unreasonable degree.

   There is a positive obsession, as in being obsessed with the Word of God, the Love of God, the Power of God, and with the things of God. This is a good thing. There is also an evil, negative obsession that can be a terrible and evil taskmaster with the capacity to destroy the human personality. An obsessed person comes to a place of having no "will power" or strength to resist, and thus he is in bondage. This is a critical stage. It is almost impossible for someone to be delivered from this stage of demon domination without assistance. In many cases of repression, a person can with a little effort and persistence come out of it in Jesus' name and be free. A person who is depressed, depending on the degree of depression, can fight through the Word, fervent prayer, praise and worship, coupled with a reminding of what the Lord has done and can do, and return to a state of happiness and be restored to the joy of the Lord and enjoy the gift of life.

In obsession this is not so. The mind gets on a track that makes thought-change virtually impossible. The person basically has no clear perspective on truth versus a lie due to loss of control of the thinking process. In obsession, the mind transposes right and wrong and good and evil, and the person can no longer distinguish the one from the other. Obsession can arise from:

- Gross deception, false teachings, believing what is out of line with the Word of God.

- Jealousy in which an idea of a person or thing preys on the mind and takes root and grows like a vine.

- Hatred, whereby one can believe that he is disliked for various reasons and begin to hate whomever or whatever he thinks hates him, developing a complex.

- Sin can become an obsession; a person may become so engrossed with his own immorality that he is blinded and cannot see anything pure or holy.

This underscores the importance of guarding the soul, for the mind is where the will is activated, and God has given us the power to will things into existence. We are never to give this power over to another person or thing. This is why hypnotism and fortune-telling are dangerous; they involve control or reshaping a person's thinking to fit another's thinking. These are controlling spirits and not of God. Alcohol and drug addictions are examples of a person's not being able to control his own will.

He might will himself never to use again when, in fact, he has lost the power to resist.

Anything that destroys the willpower of man should be avoided at all cost. The journey into the bondage of obsession begins when a person indulges in a behavior he knows is wrong and ends when he loses the power to master his will—his willpower is totally gone. This journey begins with one step. If believers want to maintain their freedom, they must be cautioned against ever taking that first step away from what they know is right. It is not impossible to be set free from obsession, for Jesus has the power to set free. In Mark 9:23, Jesus says, "If thou canst believe, all things are possible to them that believeth."

7. **Possession:** to which the devil captures the immortal soul, to inhabit; to occupy; to control; to hold as a property; to completely dominate; to actuate; to rule by extraneous forces.

Most people who become demon-possessed are totally, absolutely, and completely under the authority of the devil. This crowns Satan as master of that person's thinking and actions. Furthermore, it means that the person has no power to think of God, no spirit to reach for God, and no soul to pray to God for help. This implies that whoever has control over a person's thinking and actions had control of his life. This places the life of a possessed person in the hands of a diabolical beast.

Possession is revealed many times in the form of insanity. There can be times when the person's mind is clear and his speech concise and clear, and suddenly without warning the same person becomes animal-like, growling and hissing; this is demonic. The devil has seized this person and enslaved him to the powers of darkness. Demon possession is revealed in a person's eye; the eyes are not normal. The eyes always look away; they are shifty, glassy, squinted, or have an animal-like stare.

Another sign of possession is in spiritual discernment. If a person is filled with the Holy Spirit and a devil is within someone they meet, there is a great clash of spirits inside; it becomes a spiritual warfare of opposite spirits that is many times dismissed merely as "bad chemistry" or "personality clashes." Much demon possession results from association with people already under demonic possession.

In the other areas discussed in this section, demons were involved in the mind and the body, but not in the spirit. Demon possession means that the person has a demon or multiple demons living within his spirit. This can happen to some of the most wonderful people we know. As awful as it is, however, this is not a sickness unto death and can be conquered. Christ Jesus set the captives free 2,000 years ago, and He is the same bondage-breaker today. Deliverance comes through the same power and anointing.

Contributing Factors to the Symptoms and Manifestations of Demonization

- What are the legal and moral grounds on which the demon took up residence?
- How many demons are involved? (Mark 5)
- What kinds of demons are involved? (Matthew 12:44-45) What is the extent of their wickedness?

- The power of the demons involved (Mark 9:29).

- The purpose for their indwelling.

- The degree of compliance or consent on the part of the person indwelt.

- The permission of God.

Some of the More Severe Symptoms and Characteristics of Demonization in the Bible

- A stepping forth of a new personality in the victim; totally opposing the victim's normal personality (varying degrees).

- Extraordinary physical strength (Mark 5, Acts 19) due to a supernatural enhancement of the person by the demon powers.

- Fits of rage or extreme violent behavior are common (Mark 5:4, Matthew 8:28).

- Vocal outbursts and abusive ranting and tongue-lashing.

- Self-destructive behavior (Mark 5:5,13; Matthew 17:14-20).

- Antisocial behavior designed to humiliate the victim (Luke 8:27).

- Physical disease or disability or deformity (Matthew 9:32-34; Luke 13:20-21); this does not mean a disease is necessarily the cause of demonic influence.

- An alien voice speaking through the vocals of the victim (Mark 5, Acts 19).

- Resistance to spiritual things, especially the name of Jesus (Mark 5:7).

- An unnatural fear or phobia—an overwhelming, paralyzing fear of any sort.
- Periods of deep depression that cannot be shaken.
- Confusion in the mind; inability to think straight especially in respect to the Bible and truth.
- Restlessness, sleeplessness.
- Obscenities and profanities periodically assailing the mind unexpectedly.
- Sleepiness and unusual demand for sleep when the body should have had plenty of rest.
- Uncontrollable and unreasonable rages and temper tantrums.
- Talkativeness; rambling nonsense and confusion.
- Sudden suicidal and homicidal urges.
- Schizophrenia, sudden changes for the worse in the personality.
- Recurring headaches, fullness in the chest that makes breathing difficult, heart palpitations, pains that come and go without apparent cause and that move about over the body.
- Urges to smoke, to drink, to take drugs, to read pornography, to look at violence and bloodshed.
- An unexplained and unreasonable rebellion against authority.
- Urges toward sexual perversion of any type.
- Married person's unnatural aversion toward marital sex.
- Unusual abilities to foresee things in the future, to discern personal things about others, to perform feats of healing,

etc., when afterward the person gets depressed and bound up.

- In general, any strong urge to do something that cannot be controlled and that goes beyond the realm of the natural.

The range of manifestations is vast and varied. However, Deliverance Ministers should never be deterred by the manifestations. When deliverance is taking place, the victim is generally aware that something is occurring on the spiritual level. The person may feel embarrassed by the demons, especially if they come out with vomiting or some other obviously uncomfortable route. Deliverance Ministers should not be alarmed if the person speaks in a tone or voice out of character such as:

(1) A woman speaking with a man's voice.

(2) Adults speaking or crying like a small child.

(3) Harsh demonic tongues being spoken against you.

Demonic powers will often cause people to act out of character. It is important to immediately reassure the person that those things happen and that it is the anointing of the Holy Spirit that stirs up the demonic and initiates the process of deliverance.

Manifestations Common in Ministering Deliverance

- **Cold**—Especially when spirits associated with death or serious evil practices begin to manifest.

- **Trembling**—Either part of the body or the whole body can tremble gently.

- **Shaking**—When trembling becomes more powerful, specific parts of the body in which the demon has had a strong hold can shake, sometimes powerfully. The shaking can be so strong that the person is thrown to the ground.

- **Falling to the Ground**—In the Gospel accounts of the healing ministry of Jesus, people were thrown to the ground was recorded only when demons were encountered.

- **Palpitations**—These can cause a sense of panic in the person. This is either natural fear or a consequence of the demonic reaction of having to leave.

- **Pressure**—Especially on the head or the shoulders.

- **Physical Pain**—When a demon is forced to manifest, it will sometimes cause pain in the part of the body that it has influenced. This can be the case with spirits of infirmity or spirits that are attached to the consequences of accidents or traumas of the past.

- **Lumps in the Throat**—The most common exit point for demons is either on the breath or through the throat. It sometimes feels as though there is a physical lump when the demons are on the way out.

- **Deep Breathing**—When demons exit on the breath there is usually a deepening of the breathing cycle, which can sometimes develop into yawning or coughing. Interestingly, spirits of death usually live in the lung area.

- **Stirring in the Stomach**—A demon that has lodged in the stomach will sometimes move around shortly before deliverance takes place, giving the feeling of something going round and round in the stomach. At other times a person may feel he is going to be physically sick, although he rarely is. A type of vomiting (or retching) may take place.

- **Feeling Ill or Faint**—The experience of feeling sick can be felt in various parts of the body (especially the head) and is not just limited to the stomach area.

- **Sudden Headaches**—A common symptom, especially when dealing with mind control spirits or religious spirits or false religions and idolatry. A tight band is sometimes felt around the head, as if the demon is trying to compress the brain.

- **Unnatural Movements**—The hands, arms, legs, and feet can sometimes move wildly as demons are being expelled. On occasions, the movements betray evidence of how the demons got in. At other times, the movements may indicate release of pain at the same time as deliverance is taking place.

- **Contortions of the Body**—When spirits are coming off the spine, for example, the back can be arched backwards like the sting of a scorpion. The fetal position may also indicate long-buried pain, and it is important to discern correctly what is actually happening.

- **Screaming**—A scream will often indicate a demon leaving, but if it continues without release, there will be emotions involved that need healing.

- **Pupil Dilating**—The eye is the lamp of the body. Where light comes in, the demons may also look out. The effect can be for movements of the pupils to be independent of their normal response to light and dark as the demons manifest.

- **Squints and Convergence of the Eyeballs**—During deliverance, it is sometimes helpful to look the person (and the demons) in the eye. There is something about a look that implies authority. The demons will do all they can to avoid eye contact. The most common tactic is to make the eyes diverge or converge so that it is impossible to look into both eyes at the same time.

- **Pupils Disappearing Upwards**—When only the whites of the eye are visible, the demon has taken the eyeball upwards so that it is not possible to look the person in the eye. This power is commonly encountered when there is any form of witchcraft in evidence.

- **Sexual Movements (or feelings)**—When sexual spirits manifest they can sometimes make the person have feelings and responses in the sexual area.

- **Demonic Tongues**—Not all tongues are of the Holy Spirit. It is relatively easy to sense the harshness of a demonic tongue that is in conflict with the tongues that are a gift of the Spirit.

- **Sudden Violent Actions**—When ministering deliverance there can be a sudden violent reaction, when a particular demonic stronghold is mentioned as if it has been suddenly awakened from a long sleep. Be on your guard—especially when dealing with severely demonized people.

- **Running Away**—Sometimes people will be tempted by their demons to get up and run when the possibility of deliverance is near. People need to be encouraged to know that their bodies are their own and they do not have to obey what the demons are telling them to do.

- **Hissing**—Hissing is a characteristic of the snake. It is not surprising, therefore, that demons who are subject to "that old serpent, the devil" should manifest in this way. Hissing can also indicate spirits that imitate members of the cat family.

- **Burping**—Where demons have been present on the digestive system, there may be manifestations of burping.

- **Swearing**—People who do not normally swear at all can suddenly break out with a barrage of the foulest language when a demon is exposed and forced to the surface. Demons do not like being expelled.

- **Snarling and Barking**—These are characteristics of animals, usually dogs. Where animalistic spirits manifest, it is usually indicative of false religions, witchcraft, or Satanism having some influence on the person or his generational line.

- **Roaring**—Usually spirits of the larger cats (lions, jaguars, etc.); again, most often associated with the higher occult powers.

- **Bellowing**—sounds like an angry bull; usually evidence of strong rebellion.

- **Pungent Smells**—When some demons leave there is a nasty smell left behind. Again, this is only normally experienced when dealing with high powers of occult rituals.

- **Claw-Like Actions**—Evidence again of animalistic spirits. These spirits might have accessed the family line through bestiality or through idolatry of the animals or their images.

- **Slithering across the Floor like a Snake**—A more powerful demonstration of a snake-like spirit than hissing.

As soon as any of the above manifestations occurs, quietly exercise the authority you have in Jesus Christ and order the demon to leave without hurting either the individual or anyone else. There may be resistance, but if all the rights the demons had have been undercut, there is no reason why they will not have to leave. When dealing with severely demonized people, the controlling spirit will sometimes manifest in order to distress the person and try to terminate the ministry. This will only occur when the controlling spirit has a well-organized defense, which may have to be broken down before the stronghold can be demolished. When the defenses are down, even apparently powerful demons are reduced to size and are not stronger than others. A demon is only as strong as the defense or rights it has.

How to Know if Someone is Under a Curse

The Bible lists some 70 specific sins that could bring curses on people. Below are listed a few of the more common ones with reference to the biblical passage:

- Those who curse or mistreat the Jews fall under a curse (Genesis 12:3).

- Anybody who is a willing deceiver who keeps his sword from bloodshed or is lax in doing the Lord's work comes under a curse (Jeremiah 48:10, Judges 5:23).

- An adulterous man or woman falls under God's curse (Numbers 5:27).

- Disobedience to the Lord's commandment will lead to curses (Deuteronomy 11:28). It matters not how small the commandment is; if God says "do it" and one does not do it, he will come under a curse.

- Idolatry. Any form of idolatry brings a curse (Exodus. 20:5).

- Those who keep or own cursed objects. If you have an object or a material in your possession that God does not approve of or that is spiritually contaminated, you come under a curse (Deuteronomy 7:25-26). God does not expect us to decorate our houses with images of evil animals such as owls, vultures, cats, etc.

- If you refuse to come to the Lord's calling you will come under a curse. When God is calling for you to come and you refuse to come, the Bible says you are under a curse (Judges 5:23). When people are trying to do something for the Lord's sake, and you refuse to come out, you come under a curse.

- The house of the wicked. The Bible says the house of the wicked shall be cursed (Proverbs 3:33). If somebody comes from the house of the wicked, he will be cursed. For example, if one's parents dealt in witchcraft or visited psychics or sorcerers or dealt in the charms or the tarot cards, destroying lives and homes, the person will be delivered only if he breaks the curse. If one's father was a lodge member, the Bible says he is wicked.

- Anyone who has and does not give to the poor comes under a biblical curse (Proverbs 28:27).

- The earth is cursed because of man's disobedience (Isaiah 24:3-6).

- "Those who prefer to listen to their partners than to God also come under a curse. When God is saying something, and one's partner is saying something else, listening to the latter rather than the former will cause one to come under a curse (Genesis 3:17).

- Those who insult their parents come under a curse (Deuteronomy 27:16).

- Those who rob God of tithe and offering are under a curse (Malachi 3:9). When a person fails to pay his tithe or offering or always borrow against it or think it is too much and pay less, he is inviting God's curse.

- Those who make graven images (Deuteronomy 27:15).

- Those who willfully cheat people out of their property fall under a curse (Deuteronomy 27:17).

- Those who take advantage of the blind because they cannot see or the deaf because they cannot hear are under a curse (Deuteronomy 27:18).

- Those who lie with their fathers wife fall under a curse (Deuteronomy 27:20).

- Those who lie with beasts are under a curse (Deuteronomy 27:21).

- Anybody who lies with his own sister is under a curse (Deuteronomy 27:22).

- Those who take money to slay the innocent, including doctors who abort, come under a curse (Deuteronomy 27:25).

- The proud fall under a curse (Psalm 119:21).

- Those who trust in men and not in God fall under a curse (Jeremiah 17:5).

- Those who reward evil for good are cursed (Proverbs 17:13)

- Illegitimate children are cursed (Deuteronomy 23:2).

Signs and Effects of Curses

- Poverty, debts, failure, continuing financial insufficiency.

- Chronic sickness, torments, barrenness, miscarriages, female reproductive problems.

- Insanity, deceit, many traumatic experiences, mental and emotional breakdown, family breakdowns.

- An influx of tragedies, being accident-prone, family history of suicides and untimely deaths, calamity, torment, vexation, misfortune.

- Spiritual hindrances, domination by inferior forces, vagabondism and wandering lifestyles, abuse and mistreatment from other people.

- Abandonment by God, family breakdowns.

Recommended Practices for Breaking Curses

1. Repent from all known and unknown sins.

2. When you are asking for forgiveness, first of all ask for forgiveness for those sins that you are committing unawares.

3. Renounce all ancestral sins.

4. Accept God's forgiveness and also forgive yourself. People often find it hardest to forgive themselves.

5. Forgive all who have ever offended you.

6. Renounce all contacts with demonic religions and objects.

7. Break the curse by aggressive prayer.

8. Cast out every demon of that curse because there is always a demon that will make sure the curse works.

How Curses are Broken

All curses are broken on the basis of Galatians 3:13-14 and Colossians 2:3-15.

> *"Christ redeemed us from the curse of the law by becoming a curse for us, for it is written: 'Cursed is everyone who is hung on a tree.' He redeemed us in order that the blessing given to Abraham might come to the Gentiles through Christ Jesus, so that by faith we might receive the promise of the Spirit."* *(Galatians 3:13-14 NIV)*

> *"When you were dead in you sins and in the uncircumcision of your sinful nature, God made you alive with Christ. He forgave us all our sins, having cancelled the written code, with its regulations, that was against us and that stood opposed to us; he took it away, nailing it to the cross. And having disarmed the powers and authorities, He made a public spectacle of them, triumphing over them by the cross."* *(Colossians 2:13-15 NIV)*

Expelling Demons

Expelling demons does not involve altering a habit, a mental state, or a psychological condition. It is expelling a spiritual being. To expel means:

(1) To deprive (a person) of the membership of or involvement in (a school, society etc.);

(2) To force out or eject (a thing from its container etc.),

(3) Order or force to leave (a building, etc.).

Jesus used one-fourth of the time in His public ministry to cast out demons. Deliverance in the Bible always came before His preaching ministry. Jesus Christ knew that all believers needed to be set free and kept free of the clutches of the devil.

- Ideally, deliverance should be ministered by male to male, or female to female. But if a man prays for a female, another female or other man should be present. This removes the possibility of false accusations of sexual misconduct or other impropriety. It also ensures there is assistance in the event of physical manifestations or need for restraint.

- Paper tissues and trash containers should be on hand. Many times tears and mucus are produced when demonic powers are driven out and the emotions released.

- Whenever possible, the person should be prayed for in a private place. This spares the embarrassment of others' knowing what bondages have been broken, what dominant spirits are ejected, and seeing the display of opposition or emotion.

- The counseling sessions and the details of deliverance should be kept strictly confidential. Whatever details a person wishes to disclose about the deliverance is his personal decision alone.

- Fasting is not absolutely necessary, but may open one up to greater understanding in difficult cases or release more power in ministry.

- Everyone involved in deliverance needs to be especially sensitive to recognizing the difference between demonic oppression and psychologically-based symptoms.

- If the person is unwilling to cooperate, it is advisable not to try to minister deliverance. This should never be forced. Some people with mental problems may not be able to consent to prayer, but someone who brings them may consent on their behalf. Sometimes it is necessary to ask a person to speak out willingness to obey God in order to break the strong power of a spirit of unforgiveness, resentment, bitterness, hatred, lust, or an addictive habit.

- Persons should be seated on a straight-backed chair for easy access and control. When laying hands on a person for the breaking of bondages and expelling dominating spirits, all the people involved should stand on one side of the person receiving deliverance. This avoids being hit by any sudden lashing out with the arms and legs caused by resistance.

- Demonic powers must never be allowed to take control. The person must be restrained physically and kept from doing harm to himself, others, or property.

- In casting out demonic powers, the one ministering deliverance must operate within the boundaries of his or her capabilities. Satan will always tempt the overzealous worker to operate out of self-confidence. Demons will show their anger towards anyone operating beyond his level of faith or further afflict the person being helped.

- Avoid a demonic "talk back show." Demons lie and cannot be trusted.

- Be confident in God's authority, and use it as if you were Jesus himself.

Maintaining Spiritual Freedom

Maintaining spiritual freedom is not easy for a person who has been set free from bondage. The devil is an expert at attempting to regain entrance into the life of that person. In many instances, the person has no real concept of what or how he came to the point of being demonized. The person ministering deliverance needs to offer encouragement and assistance to the newly-delivered believer. After deliverance, nurturing and providing answers to questions that may arise is part of post-deliverance counseling. In post-deliverance counseling, failure to teach people to walk in maturity and full victory makes them susceptible to more deception and renewed attacks. Newly-delivered believers are often assaulted by the enemy as he attempts to regain control in their lives; the enemy does not take defeat lightly. Listed are points from Evicting Demonic Intruders (Gibson & Gibson, 1993) for people who have been freed:

1. Declare aloud in prayer, positively and gratefully, the major areas in which you have received freedom.

    For example: "Thank You, Lord, for taking away my rejection / my low self-image / my anger / my lust / my bondage to Satan / the memory of my past, etc."

    Never offer to Satan the keys of doubt or negative thinking. Without hesitation, he will use them to oppress you. Remember:

- God's forgiveness and cleansing give you self-acceptance.
- God's restoration and renewal give you self-respect.
- God's boundless love, joy, and peace give you self-worth.

2. Commence each new day and continue through each day by making right and positive choices.

   Never let your feelings dictate your behavior because they can be deceptive. Jesus Christ has called you to discipleship, which means denying yourself, taking up your cross, and following Him (Matthew 16:24). Discipleship brings the knowledge of truth, and truth sets us free (John 8:31-32). Spirit-filled living is based on right choices.

   - Right choices release faith and control feelings.
   - Right choices will discipline the flesh and bring it under control. The flesh can never be cast out, but it can be subject to the lordship of Christ (Romans 8:12-17).
   - Right choices give glory to God; obedience reveals our love for Him.

3. Expect continuous and increasing freedom in areas where Satan has previously exploited you.

   When the Hebrews came out of Egypt, a minority kept complaining about God's diet of manna. They had memories about the delicacies they had left behind (i.e., when they were in bondage and enslaved). God became exasperated with their grumbling and fed them quail flesh for breakfast, lunch, and dinner, served with plague (Numbers 11). What caused their problems? Living in the past instead of looking forward to all God had promised for the new life. From the time of experiencing freedom, there must be no more post-mortems but rather a reaching forward to all that God has in store.

4. Never forget that the devil is an incorrigible liar.

He is a liar by profession, and he is highly skilled at it (John 8:44). Everything he whispers in your ear will turn out to be sugar-coated poison aimed at your defeat. Should he counter-attack after deliverance, trying to convince you that you were not really free at all (because it was only a psychological or emotional trick), reject the suggestion and him. Your shield of faith will preserve you from those fiery darts. When John Wesley, the founder of Methodism, was supposedly confronted by the devil with pages of his past wrongdoings, he told him to write all over them in red ink: "The blood of Jesus Christ, God's Son, cleanses me from all sin." The devil then made a hasty exit. Resist the devil but avoid conversing with demons, particularly if you have been hearing voices. Resist them by the shield of faith, then concentrate on praising God for the completeness and permanency of the freedom He purchased for you at Calvary. Let the Spirit of God renew your mind, and keep it renewed.

5. Remember that Jesus Christ has freed you from all condemnation (Romans 8:1).

The devil will try to make you stumble over some misunderstanding or imaginary hurt. Then, when you have lost your balance, he will push you down the slide of discouragement. At the bottom, the spiritual bullies of guilt and condemnation are waiting to pummel you. Then someone will have to drag you up that hill again. It could all have been avoided by refusing to allow anything to come between Jesus Christ and yourself.

No one was more misunderstood and had more hurts than Jesus, yet He refused all self-pity. Live in His freedom. There is an old saying: "You can't stop birds from flying over your head, but you can stop them from nesting in your hair." The moral is to refuse to accept doubt and discouragement and you won't be filled with condemnation. Stop those destructive thoughts before they have a chance to nest! Claim your blood-sealed rights, and reject even the fear of condemnation.

6. Don't play with deliberate sin; it is a poisonous snake.

Believers are forbidden to sin deliberately. But should you unintentionally sin repent and confess it immediately so that you can receive forgiveness and cleansing. Remember:

- God expects us to live holy (set apart). "Be holy, for I am holy" (Leviticus 11:44-45).

- Guilt is the shadow cast by sin. When the cause is removed there is no longer any basis for guilt. Don't fool yourself or let the evil one stand between you and the Light.

- Never save sin up for a later confession: Like dirty clothes in a hamper, have spiritual contamination removed immediately.

- Don't generalize your confession of sin such as "Lord, forgive my sins." Itemize them, name them, name each horrible thought or act separately. God requires genuine repentance.

- Never leave the presence of God without consciously receiving His cleansing. Go away free of defilement, burdens, guilt, stain, and know you are beyond condemnation.

7. Invite the Holy Spirit to enable you to make Jesus Lord of your entire personality every day.

    The act of consecration in Romans 12 is threefold:

    - What you give to God is yourself—your whole self: body, mind, and spirit; all your thoughts, behaviors, and feelings. In other words, Lordship means the willing subjection of spirit, soul, and body to the Spirit of God (Romans 12:2).

    - What you receive from God is a renewed mind able to understand and carry out the will of God (Romans 12:2).

    - What you do for God is fulfill what He has appointed you to do within the Body of Christ (Romans 12:3-8), and bless His world (Romans 12:9-21). God is not asking you to fit the Kingdom of God into your objectives. Your life should be a means God uses for fulfilling His objectives. The moral evidence of living a victorious life is the witness of being filled and controlled by the Holy Spirit.

8. Make time to read, learn, and meditate on God's Word and communicate with Him constantly.

    Probably the first casualty of an over-busy lifestyle is our two-way communication with God. Bible reading, prayer, meditation, and worship are our spiritual food and breath. Satan tolerates Christians as long as they skimp on spiritual necessities. He fears their having

God's wisdom and strength or finding out His subtleties. The old saying still holds: "Either God's Word will keep you from sin, or sin will keep you from God's Word."

- God said to Joshua:
  "Do not let this Book of the Law depart from your mouth; meditate on it day and night, so that you may be careful to do everything written in it. Then you will be prosperous and successful" (Joshua 1:8).

- The Psalmist said:
  "How can a young man keep His way pure? By living according to your word. I seek you with all my heart; Do not let me stray from your commands I have hidden your word in my heart That I might not sin against you." (Psalm 119:9-11)

- Paul said:
  "Study and be eager and do your utmost to present yourself to God approved (tested by trial), a workman who has no cause to be ashamed, correctly analyzing and accurately dividing-rightly and handling and skillfully teaching the Word of Truth" (2 Timothy 2:15, AMP).

9. Put on, or affirm, the protection of the armor of God daily.

    God's spiritual armor is both offensive and defensive against Satan's attacks (Ephesians 6:10-18). The Apostle Paul, who appeared to have had more demonic opposition than his fellow apostles, described each item needed to cope with the assaults of demonic beings. Each article was first tested and proved by Jesus Christ in defeating every demonic power (Hebrews 2:17-18). The power to withstand Satan and to remain standing when the attack is over comes from prayer directed and energized by the Holy Spirit (Ephesians 6:18).

10. Train yourself to be constantly thankful and full of praise. *"Praise the Lord, O my soul, and forget not all His benefits" (Psalm 103:2).*

Praise disturbs the enemy. When King Jehoshaphat found that the Moabites and Ammonites had declared war on him, he called his people together and asked God for help. The prophet Jahaziel then said:

"This is what the Lord says to you: Do not be afraid or discouraged because of this vast army. For the battle is not yours, but God's... You will not need to fight in this battle. Take up your positions; stand firm and see the deliverance the Lord will give you" (2 Chronicles 20:15,17).

Never be ungrateful for what God has done for you. Your song of gratitude will be a warning to Satan to back off from any takeover he might have in mind. He fears a praising saint.

Finally, draw on your available spiritual resources after receiving a major deliverance. It is possible for another demonic manifestation to occur, possibly because a bondage that was overlooked at the time of ministration has now come to light as a result of the new work of grace within you.

CHAPTER 8

Biblical Spiritual Warfare

Weapons and Methods of Spiritual Warfare

SPIRITUAL WARFARE is a term used to describe intangible conflict and infliction of assaults. These emanate from and take place in the invisible, spiritual realm of creation. Christians are God's soldiers, and the warfare they wage is not physical but spiritual, fought on spiritual principles with spiritual weapons and methods. These weapons are not only defensive but offensive as well. No army can win a battle with defensive measures alone. They must also carry out offensive attacks.

Defensive measures alone leave the believer open for the enemy to plan the next attack without opposition. Believers must fight back to win so that the enemy will be confused about the next point of attack. Colossians 2:15 states, *"And having spoiled principalities and powers, he made a shew of them openly, triumphing over them in it."* Jesus spoiled principalities and powers, and made an open show of them. He not only won the battle but put the enemy on display.

The hallmark of biblical spiritual warfare is Ephesians 6:12:

> *"For we wrestle…against principalities, against powers, against the rulers of darkness of this world."*

The believer's approach to spiritual warfare should be based on biblical doctrine. Subjective feelings, emotional desires, and sincerity are not sufficient weapons against Satan (Prince, 2006).

He does not bow to emotions or feelings. He yields only to the believer's authority through the blood of Jesus Christ and the absolute truth of the Word of God. We cannot defeat the enemy with fervent emotion; His defeat is in our relying on the Word of God and the Person and work of the Holy Spirit. Because of our relationship to God, we are targets for attack from the same enemy who attacked the person, plans, and purposes of Jesus Christ. With these powerful forces against us, it is to our benefit to know all that we can about our offensive and defensive "weapons of spiritual warfare." It is vital that believers become familiar with spiritual warfare and become good soldiers of Jesus Christ; this involves recognizing the attacks, temptations, and testing from Satan and responding accordingly.

Ephesians 6: The New Testament Manual on Spiritual Warfare

Paul begins his presentation on spiritual warfare in Ephesians 6:10-18 (NIV) with the word:

> "Finally, be strong in the Lord and in the strength of
> His might."

This is an empowering charge to believers that their strength to withstand the attacks is in their relationship with the Lord. We must stand and believe in the power and strength of God.

> "Put on the full armor of God, so that you can take
> your stand against the devil's schemes."

A strong belief in God together with an iron clad spiritual armor will lead to a total destroying of the works of Satan. We must first be able to stand against the attacks of Satan by getting fully equipped with His armor that prepares us to engage in battle against the enemy's schemes.

"For or struggle is not against flesh and blood, but against the rulers, against the authorities, against the power of this dark world and against the spiritual forces of evil in the heavenly realms."

The fight is not with flesh; the fight is with disembodied spirits, and they are real and endued with powers of darkness. Their goal is to defeat the Church of Jesus Christ. Paul lists the battle armor the believer must don in Ephesians 6:13-18:

"Therefore put on the full armor of God, so that when the day of evil comes, you may be able to stand your ground, and after you have done everything to stand."

This is a second warning to stress the importance of putting on the full armor of God before engaging in the warfare. The first thing to do in warfare is to be trained. Discipline and training enable the believer to stand when the struggles become fierce. Each piece of armor represents a specific truth. Ephesians 6:14 lists the first piece of armor:

"Stand firm then, with the belt of truth buckled around your waist, with the breastplate of righteousness in place."

The girdle, or belt, of truth requires that we hold tight to ourselves (in our hearts) the precious truth of the Word of God without doubt or compromise and renounce every lie that the enemy uses to deceive us. In doing this, we are protected by the breastplate of righteousness. Romans 10:10 states: "For with the heart one believes unto righteousness." This protects our hearts because we have the righteousness of Christ.

"And with your feet fitted with the readiness that comes from the gospel of peace."

Good footwear enables swift, sturdy movement. This gives one the motivation to continue in the Gospel in peace, taking firm, strong steps and moving in a forward motion.

> *"In addition to all of this, take up the shield of faith, with which you can extinguish all the flaming arrows of the evil one."*

Our shield of faith must be complete in all its dimensions. It must cover our total personality, spirit, soul, and body. We must also be so spiritually fit that we are completely covered by the promises of God. When Satan launches those fiery arrows aimed to kill us, the shield of our faith will not just stop them, but quench them, "extinguishing the flames."

> *"Take the Helmet of Salvation and the Sword of the Spirit, which is the Word of God."*

The helmet protects the mind and thoughts. The mind is an area where Christians are often attacked because it is the seat of thought and the battleground for all of man's spiritual concerns. The idea here is to fill the mind with the Word of God; this is protection. Otherwise, the devil will fill the mind with his thoughts. Meditate on scriptures. Learn scripture by heart. This is how to keep the mind fixed on the Word of God and keep the enemy at bay.

Sword of the Spirit

A sword is a thrusting, striking, or cutting weapon with a long blade with one or two cutting edges. It is a weapon of offense and is used to attack an enemy. Up to this point, we have examined the weapons of defense designed to protect us from the enemy. The sword must be used in offense as well as defense, both to fight the enemy and to fend off attacks. The presentation proceeds from defense to offense because believers must be secure in their defense before attempting to engage in an attack lest they be unprepared for the enemy's counterattack. An old sports axiom has it that "The best defense is a good offense." Merely having a Bible is not what is effective. But when believers have the Word of God in their mouths and proclaim it boldly then it becomes a two-edged sword. It is the Holy Spirit who actually wields it.

> *"And pray in the spirit on all occasions with all kinds*
> *of prayers and requests. With this in mind, be alert*
> *and always keep on praying for all the saints."*

Ephesians 6:18 teaches believers how to pray, when to pray, the type of prayers to pray, and what to pray for:

a. Praying to God (Hebrews 11:6)

b. Praying in the name of Jesus (John 14:6)

c. Praying in the Spirit (Ephesians 6:18)

d. Praying according to the will of God (1 John 5:14-15)

e. Praying in faith (Ephesians 3:20; James 1:6)

f. Praying earnestly (Luke 6:12)

g. Praying without hypocrisy (Matthew 6:5)

Of the other spiritual defenses of armor with which believers fight, this is a weapon without boundaries or limitations. Prayer is our weapon of mass destruction. Focused prayer directed by the Holy Spirit can transcend countries, continents, and oceans and strike with unprecedented accuracy. Prayer encompasses all of the following listed in 1 Timothy 2:1:

• **Supplications**—personal needs

• **Prayers**—petitions

• **Intercessions**—interceding on the behalf of others

• **Giving of thanks**—praise and worship

This is the most powerful weapon, yet many Christians are weak in prayer. Persistent prayer as a weapon produces outstanding results. Daniel prayed for 21 days and refused to cease until he received the answer. The angel knew that Daniel was still praying when he responded that Daniel's prayer was answered on the first day. At times, however, the messengers of God have to fight to bring the answers. The answers to prayers leave the third heaven where God is, pass through the second heaven (which is the high places where the principalities and powers of darkness reside), then return to the earth to be delivered to the children of God. And the process is reversed as the angel planned his departure to return to the heavenlies.

The Bible gives examples of another weapon of warfare—Praise. Psalm 22:23 states:

> *"Ye that fear the Lord praise him, all ye the seed of Jacob glorify him; and fear him, all ye the seed of Israel."*

In the book of Acts, when Paul and Silas began to praise God, their chains broke and they were set free.

Another weapon for fighting the enemy is the blood of Jesus. Revelation 12:11 states:

> *"And they overcame him by the blood of the Lamb and by the word of their testimony, and they loved not their lives unto the death. There is power in the blood of Jesus. When you plead the blood of Jesus, No demon will be able to touch you because of the power in the blood of Jesus. And when we sing songs about the blood of Jesus we are singing powerful songs because the blood is responsible for our redemption, forgiveness, cleansing, justification and sanctification."*

Another spiritual weapon is the Fire of God. Hebrews 12:29 states:

> *"For our God is a consuming fire. He will consume the works of the devil."*

Psalms 104:4 states:

> *"Who maketh his angels spirits; His ministers a flaming fire."*

God can turn a believer into a flaming fire so that when someone attempts to touch him with the intent of doing harm he will be touching fire.

One of the most effective measures Christians use in spiritual warfare is wielding "the Sword of the Spirit" by the power of Holy Ghost to engage in spiritual warfare against:

- **The Flesh**—This is the greatest battle the believer has in spiritual warfare. The flesh cannot be cast out or delivered; it must be crucified. If there is a demon in the flesh, the demon can be cast out, but the flesh must be brought up under the subjection of the Spirit. One must learn to listen to the Holy Spirit. The enemy uses man's flesh by to tempt and war against the spiritual man. The flesh is deadly and capable of defeating believers and keeping them from pleasing God. Before conversion, the flesh actually controlled man's inner life.

  Fleshly sins cannot be blamed on Satan or the world or anything but the self. Satan may generate the tempting thoughts; however, the believer has a choice not to act on the thought or bring it to fruition. The flesh is intimately entwined with our minds, will, and emotions. The flesh works closely with man's personality, the self-satisfying sources of pleasure, as well as pain and worldly perception. The word flesh (Greek: sarx) is one of the most commonly used terms in the New Testament to identify man's inherited fallen nature.

Mark Bubeck, in his book The Adversary, defines the flesh as:

"The flesh is a built-in law of failure, making it impossible for natural man to please or serve God. It is a compulsive inner force inherited from mans fall, which expresses itself in general and specific rebellion against God and His righteousness. The flesh can never be reformed or improved. The only hope for escape from the law of the flesh is its total execution and replacement by a new life in the Lord Jesus Christ."

In order to be successful in Spiritual Warfare it is paramount that believers become familiar with their own temptations, face them truthfully, understand their source, and know God's remedy for the problem. The flesh is a strong force within us, and even after we have by faith counted him dead, he attempts to spring back to life and control us. The flesh can never be changed or improved; the only hope for escape from the law of the flesh is in the total execution and replacement by a new life in the Lord Jesus Christ.

This is warfare in the flesh. Galatians 5:19-21 gives us a comprehensive list of fleshly sins.

"Now the works of the flesh are manifest, which are these; adultery, fornication, uncleanness, lasciviousness. Idolatry, witchcraft, hatred, variance, emulations, wrath, strife, seditions, heresies, envying, murders, drunkenness, revellings, and such like of the

which I tell your before, as I have also told you in time past, that they which do such things shall not inherit the kingdom of God."

Deliverance is in the kingdom of God. Jesus said (Matthew 12:28):

"If I by the spirit of God could cast out the devil, then know that the kingdom of God has come among you."

Believers are also to use the "Sword of the Spirit" as a method in warfare against these other main entities:

- **Against the World**—Believers are to use the sword of the Spirit against the world. The Bible says we are in this world, but not of this world.

- **Against Principalities**—Believers are to use the sword of the Spirit against evil authorities, evil dominions, and rulers of darkness.

- **Against Diseases**—Believers are to use the sword of the Spirit against all diseases, demons, and every evil name.

Binding & Loosing

Another measure to use in spiritual warfare is the power of binding and loosing. Binding the strongman is a biblical method used to fight against the powers of darkness. Binding is to restrain, force, or restrict a thing. According to Matthew 18:18, binding is a legal decree or declaration on behalf of Jesus who sits at the right hand of God as judge of the heavens and the earth.

Jesus instructs believers to bind up the strongman because they cannot spoil the strongman's house unless they first bind him up. Matthew 12:29:

"Or else how can one enter into a strong man's house, and spoil his goods, except he first bind the strong-man? And then he will spoil his house."

Unless you bind the strongman, you will experience problems in casting out the lesser demons.

Loosing is another method that means releasing the yoke or foothold by breaking the power. This is to loose the effects, the signs, and symptoms associated with the evil spirit and its presence.

Exercising Believer's Authority

Another method is the exercising of the believer's authority, the authority vested in the believer by Jesus that gives believers the right to use power.

Anointing

Another method is being anointed or covered with the oil of God's anointing for divine service, being anointed for ministry and power.

Hands & Feet

Another method is the use of hands and feet. Psalm 144:1 states:

"Blessed be the Lord my strength, which teaches my hands to war, and my fingers to fight."

This means that the hands are weapons, and they can fight for one's life when the Lord is his strength. The hand is used to transfer power and blessings with the laying on of hands. The hand is the equipment of deliverance and healing. The enemy will recognize that the hands are weapons of war even when the believer does not. An example is David in 1Samuel 17:50:

> *"So David prevailed over the Philistine with a sling
> and with a stone, and smote the Philistine, and slew
> him; but there was no sword in the hand of David."*

The feet are a symbol of dominion.

> *"You shall tread upon serpents and scorpion and
> upon every power of the enemy, and nothing shall
> any means hurt you." (Luke 10:19)*

> *"And how shall they preach, except they be sent? As it
> is written: 'How beautiful are the feet that preach the
> gospel of peace, and bring glad tidings of good
> things.'" (Romans 10:15)*

It is believed that every organ in the physical body has spiritual significance and symbolism. Because mankind is in the image of God, rationally and spiritually speaking, man is God's representative on earth. This qualifies human being to be used as instruments of God for service in the kingdom of God. This service can take various forms. It can manifest as teaching corrective lessons, or as blessing God's people, or simply to use instruments of spiritual warfare to fight the enemies of God. By His grace, God gives His people these gifts as an honor and privilege.

In *The Prophet's Dictionary*, Price (2002) lists the symbolic and spiritual uses for the different organs of the body:

- **Head**—symbol in the Bible associated with wisdom, control, and authority

- **Heart**—the seat of human emotion, affections, desires, love

- **Hand**—an instrument of work, service, and spirituality

- **Eyes**—spiritual or natural presence; the lamp of the body, they reflect the inner power of a person

- **Feet**—foundation, power, vehicle of mobility , path

- **Fingers**—spiritual outreach and activity, support
- **Arm**—extension of power and representative of action, work, labor
- **Face**—an expression of confrontation
- **Legs**—represent pillars, support beams, extensions
- **Breast**—motherhood, protection, nurturing
- **Neck**—the part between the head and shoulders where the expression of will are exemplified; strength of will

The Bible says God has crowned man with glory and honor and has put him in dominion over the works of his hands. This is a position of supreme authority and responsibility over the matters of the earth. Man is God's delegated authority here on earth and represents God's interests in this world.

Power of God—Through Spiritual Warfare

Spiritual Warfare

The power of God through spiritual warfare involves reaching a mature level of spiritual understanding and authority. This includes the ability to see with spiritual insights and draw connections between things of the spirit with the understanding of the mind. It is the intelligent flowing together of knowledge and understanding to comprehend life and its wisdom. Spiritual understanding distinguishes itself by immediately apprehending and sizing up situations and circumstances, to consider the most prudent course of action. Spiritual understanding comes from God's wisdom and exceeds human and secular wisdom. Spiritual understanding includes and exalts the spiritual over the natural and operates in spiritual warfare through the revelatory spiritual gifts, such as word of wisdom, word of knowledge, and discerning of spirits.

Spiritual authority is a form of spiritual power in which believers are to operate under the authority of Jesus Christ. It is recognized both by God and by the enemy as flowing from believers, and it serves the purposes of God. The power of the Holy Spirit is the ultimate power in spiritual warfare, and the enemy cannot overcome or wrestle with deity. Christians are to align their will with the will of Jesus and exercise the authority He has given them. This alignment comes about from spending time in prayer and fellowship with God and listening to get instructions for the specific task ahead. No created power has the ability to be a barrier against the Lord Jesus. He increases the strength and power of all means as He pleases, according to His own counsel. God has the knowledge and wisdom to direct His power and execute the results of His wisdom. He knows what is good and he orders it and has the power to effect the outcome of all spiritual warfare.

Spiritual battles are more aggressive and dangerous than physical ones because these diabolical battles involve power encounters with an enemy devoid of all natural senses. He has no physical body in which to function and thus operates through the natural senses of mankind. This gives him an advantage that humans must compensate for. This compensation has to occur in a spiritual manner revealed by a higher, more knowledgeable spiritual power. Thus, in the natural realm, humans have no knowledge or understanding of the enemy bent on their destruction. They must rely, rather, on spiritual insights revealed by God's Word and Holy Spirit. The Word of God tells us that the enemy is real; he is spiritual; and he operates from the spiritual realm.

Spiritual warfare involves a demonstration of the Holy Spirit manifested in the earth through the lives of believers. Power is the ability to do something by virtue of strength, skill, resources, or authority. Satan is not willing to relinquish his hold on God's people who have accepted Christ as Lord. He refuses to allow the release of God's blessings and the souls of mankind without a battle. Thus, there will be no victory for God's people without a confrontation with the evil one. Satan's goal is to destroy the believer. If the believer gives in without resistance, Satan will gladly take him into captivity. Many Christians fail to realize that, whether they fight or not, the war has been declared and the battle is on and the enemy is very determined, experienced, and well-organized. The amount of information a believer has about the battle and the enemy will determine the outcome of the battle in his or her life. When believers are ignorant of satanic devices, they give the enemy a great advantage. The enemy will do his utmost to win, and he will surely prey on ignorance and lack of understanding.

The power of God works when the people of God are set free. This is why it is futile to attempt to engage in spiritual warfare without the Holy Spirit. Believers are to be fully confident and reassured that they are not fighting from the losing side of the battle but from a victorious position in Christ Jesus. Christ overcame the enemy and has equipped believers with the power, right, authority, to overcome him. There are many different powers in this world; some are from spiritual forces of darkness, and some are from man and his creative abilities, but there is only one Divine Power that is greater than all other powers—the power of God. Every power that is not of God is no match for the omnipotence of God.

Both the Kingdom of God and the kingdom of Satan operate in a form of hierarchical order that moves from lower ranks to the higher ranks of order (Williams, 2002). The Godhead operates with God the Father, God the Son, and God the Holy Spirit in that order. The angels of God also operate in rankings with various degrees of authority rising from the lower angels and higher angels in that rank and order. Colossians 1:16-17 lays out the order:

> *"For by Him all things were created that are in heaven and that are on earth, visible and invisible, whether thrones or dominions or principalities or powers. All things were created through Him and for Him."*

God has angelic thrones with delegated authority in various ranks according to their duties. For example, the archangel Michael is referred to as one of the Chief Princes. Daniel 10:13 states:

> *"But the Prince of Persia withstood me for twenty-one days; and behold Michael one of the chief princes came to help me, for I had been left there alone with the kings of Persia."*

The satanic hierarchy is mentioned in the Bible as well. Ephesians 6:12 states:

> *"For we do not wrestle against flesh and blood, but against principalities and powers, against the rulers of darkness of this age, against spiritual hosts of wickedness in the heavenly places."*

Satan has nothing associated with him but evil and because he is not creative, he can only offer counterfeits. He has sought to duplicate the divine order of God with a rival setup to carry out his evil works. The diabolically-erected structure of the kingdom

of Satan according to rank is listed here along with their evil as-
signments:

- **Principalities:** These are princes of the underworld who manipulate certain areas of the world. They are Ruling Spirits assigned over nations and cities and are the high-est-ranking operatives in the enemy's domain.

- **Powers:** This is the second level of authority and power in Satan's kingdom. Powers can influence the thought and feelings of human beings. They can influence people to kill, steal, and indulge in all manner of destructive deeds. Powers influence Christians to believe lies and get into a state of offense.

- **Rulers of Darkness:** This is the third level or rank in the satanic hierarchy—Rulers of Darkness of this age. These rulers are mandated by the devil to promote false religions and occult practices, thereby enslaving the souls of men in deception. Their main goal is control. They promote false teachings, false visions and dreams, astrology, numerol-ogy, palmistry, fortune telling, divinations, horoscope, hypnotism, witchcraft, black and white magic.

- **Spiritual Hosts of Wickedness:** After the Rulers of Dark-ness come the spiritual hosts of wickedness on heavenly realms. They promote lawlessness and wickedness on the earth to ensnare the souls of men into all manner of abominable sins and all manner of lusts, sexuality, lascivi-ousness, suicides, drug addictions, and others. The key to their operations is in the word "wickedness." Witches and witchcraft operations are under this group as well. Spiri-tual hosts of wickedness are responsible for accidents, pre-mature death, and delay the blessings of God's people through situations and circumstances that are orchestrated against them.

What the Bible says about power is summed up in four headings:

- ### The Unlimited Power of God

  God is Almighty and all other power is derived from and subject to Him. Much of what the Bible says about the power of God is summed up in the words of David in 1 Chronicles 29:11-12:

  > *"Thine, O Lord, is the greatness, and the power, and the glory and the victory, and the majesty; for all that is in the heavens and in the earth is thine; thine is the kingdom, O Lord... thou rulest over all. In thy hand are power and might; and in thy hand it is to make great and to give strength to all."*

- ### The Limited Power God Gives to His Creatures

  Animals have power, as it is particularly evident in the wild ox, the horse, and the lion (Job 39:11).

  There is power in wind and storm, thunder and lightning. Power is given to humans: physical strength, power to fight, and the power to do good and the power to do harm. Rulers have God-given power and authority. The Bible also speaks of the power of angels and of spiritual beings known as "principalities and powers"; certain powers are given to Satan. Sin, evil, and death are allowed to have some power over men. All of these have limited power, and God is able to give His people strength to conquer all these powers.

- ### The Power of God seen in Jesus Christ

The Gospels and the book of Acts bear frequent witness to the power of Christ. Power was shown in His miracles and in His works of healing and deliverance. Power is shown supremely in His resurrection. Jesus speaks of His power to give up His life and power to take it again.

- **The Power of God in the Lives of His People**
  In the Old Testament it is often said that the weak are made strong by the power of God. He empowers those who are weak (Isaiah 40:29) so that they may increase from strength to strength. We read of His power being given to prophets and kings, and it is said that in an outstanding way power will be given the Messiah (Isaiah 9:6, 11:2). But God offers power to all that they may live for Him and serve Him (Isaiah 49:5). When we read the gospel as the power of God for salvation to everyone who has faith (Romans 1:16), "To all who received him, who believed in his name, he gave power to become children of God" (John 1:12).

  God's purposes put our authority with God's power and make us effective through Jesus Christ. Jesus commanded people to be healed and made whole. We are to imitate Jesus and take authority as He did. The spirit world cannot turn a deaf ear to the commands of God's servants, just as we know God hears us when we speak to Him. We can be sure that the entire spirit world is listening when we direct our words that way. Any command we utter that relates to the activity of enemy spirits will be heard by them loud and clear. Our authority gives us the ability to use the power God gives us through the indwelling of the Holy Spirit. When the Holy Spirit dwells within us, the power of God is invested in us and we have the full authority of Jesus to use it. The Holy Spirit is not a gift of Power. The Holy Spirit is God Himself. God does not come to present us with a gift of power and then leave us to go out and manifest the characteristic of power.… God comes to present us with Him, His power is with Him.

There is a point in the life of every believer when Satan will bring resistance to his Christian walk. This is always an act of spiritual warfare. The whole Christian life involves spiritual warfare and will occasionally involve power encounters. Casting out demons always involves power encounters; however, power encounters do not always involve casting out demons. Power encounters can be equated with miracles, signs and wonders, truth encounters, or any event where the kingdom of God confronts the kingdom of this world. Power encounters occur with Christians and non-Christians. The Christian level is the level in which the encounter occurs and when the people of God are directly or indirectly involved.

Power Encounter: Through Spiritual Warfare from a Warrior Perspective Involves

- Being strengthened through spiritual disciplines that prepare the believer in battle according to his faith. It is the knowledge of God's Word that prevents Satan from using his tactics to entangle them in his snares.

- Putting aside passive attitudes towards faith, which tend to benefit the believer alone; keeps the believer from seeking his own agenda and promotes submission of his will to God because He calls one to make a sacrifice. This may

be to actively engage when people are in spiritual bondage.

- Having the propensity to test a situation and determine .
whether there is something more than natural influences
at work.

- Having alertness to the activity of the enemy, devoid of
fear or paranoia.

- Giving no credence to Satanic hosts for every calamity
that happens in the natural and spiritual realm, but ac-
knowledges that "the Spirit of Truth" operates in the natural and spiritual realm and Jesus is Lord of all.

- Bringing discipline to one's thoughts and to your actions.
If these areas are compromised, one cannot be effective in
resisting the enemy.

- Believers taking sin very seriously, knowing that sin always give the enemy the advantage.

- Always guarding oneself against comparisons with others,
for Jesus is our standard; this diminishes the chances of
being entrapped by the subtlety of religious pride.

—Deborah W. Nelson

CHAPTER 9

Encouragement & Counsel for Deliverance Ministers

My MAIN OBJECTIVE in researching and writing this book on Deliverance Ministry was to demystify this commonly misunderstood ministry of the Church, dispel fears associated with it, and equip Deliverance Ministers with the knowledge and skills needed to practice this very challenging ministry. To that end, I presented Deliverance Ministry as based on biblical principles interpreted and applied by orthodox Bible teachers and Deliverance Ministers. A thorough examination of scriptural teachings revealed (1) the need for Deliverance Ministry in the broad context of spiritual warfare and (2) the tragic consequences on the overall well-being of the Body of Christ of not providing Deliverance Ministry. I exposed the nature of fighting a spiritual enemy operating within the parameters of a physical body.

Though biblical knowledge is not the only qualifying factor for ministering deliverance, it is essentially the guidebook for Deliverance Ministers because is the single-most important weapon in spiritual warfare and contains the truth of the Word of God. Faith is the substance that brings the evidence of the power and authority of God. Deliverance is merely the evidence of the truth of Word of God working to set captives free by the power of the blood of Jesus Christ and through the power of the Holy Spirit.

The Church has an obligation to embrace the whole "Deliverance Plan of God."

As Christians today experience intensified evil and debauchery in the world, and ultimately within their own families and households. The need for Deliverance Ministry is as great as ever. The evidence for the existence of evil and personal enemies of the believer (devil and demons) is overwhelming. The reality of Deliverance Ministry and the need for personal deliverance becomes a greater reality when it hits close to home. As this study reveals, the fact that a person is a Christian does not imply that he or she does not commit such sins as drug abuse, swearing, gambling, or drinking alcohol.

Many believers are under the assumption that they are good people, and, perhaps by world standards, they are very kind, generous, law-abiding citizens. This is a clever deception born out of the lies of a self-righteous devil designed to keep Christians in bondage. This kind of thinking has the potential to cause people to believe that they can be good within their own power without God. As we see in the comprehensive study of manifestations and symptoms, many times believers struggle in internal areas not often spoken about in Christian settings.

Christians are sanctified—called out and set apart. Christians separated from the world are free of the world's opinions, values, pressures, and enticements. The world order is controlled by Satan, and there is a distinct line drawn between the two opposing forces, in the form of the blood of Jesus and the devil's efforts to conceal the power of the cross. The Christian life is one committed to being delivered and governed by the Word of God. The expectation is to be eternally delivered, rescued, and saved through the shed blood of Jesus Christ.

Throughout this book a theme arises: God is a deliverer, and His plan is to deliver the Church from ungodliness to godliness. A Christian is a person who has been delivered; this is the power of the cross. Many are deceived about their spiritual condition. Many believe in Jesus, and believe many things about Him to be truth, but deny the power of the cross, which is the power to bring drastic change through deliverance. Matthew 7:22-23 states:

> *"Many will say to me in that day, Lord, Lord, have we not prophesied in thy name? and in thy name have cast out devils? And in thy name done many wonderful works? And then will I profess unto them, 'I never knew you; depart from me you workers of iniquity.'"*

The "Church Today" lives between "Calvary and Today," a reality not readily addressed. It is the responsibility of the people of God to demonstrate the victory on Calvary's cross in their lives and in the lives of others by witnessing and serving in love. The truth is Jesus' blood declares deliverance, and the tools of power have been supplied and released for the use of His people. The purpose of ministering deliverance is not about demons; it is about the cross. Jesus alone had the authority and power to end Satan's rule over this world. Deliverance is a part of the atonement and the New Covenant for the believers. It is about the Body of Christ's experiencing, as well as bringing others, spiritual victory and freedom from bondage. It does not matter if the bondage be called demonized, depressed, possessed, oppressed, demonic influence, etc., it is still bondage from which one needs to be delivered in order to enjoy the abundant life Christ came to bring. The objective is to set the captives free and expose the truth of God's Word.

184 / I Declare War

It is critical to dispel the common myth among believers that casting out demons is the overall ministry of deliverance. As revealed in the fundamentals of Christian deliverance, human being comprises body, soul, and spirit, and it is possible for a person to be in need of deliverance in any area of a Christian's life (or all of them). Many Christians do not realize just how the enemy assaults them in social, spiritual, financial, and every other aspect of everyday life.

The problem is that we must expose the enemy at all costs. He is a deceiver, and the greatest deception is to hide his evil deeds by persuading Christians not to expose him. Much of the emotional and spiritual demonic activity operating in believers' lives is oblivious to them. Demons do not enter in an instant; in most cases they are developed in the early stages of life and manifest at some time in adulthood.

Many in the Body of Christ believe that Christians cannot have a demon or demonic influence in their life, while believing that they can have sin in their life. Many times Jesus cast out demons for the people in the synagogues, as in Mark 1:39: "And he preached in their synagogues throughout all Galilee, and cast out devils."

Sin and demonic activity are in fellowship together, which is why the Church has a grave need for Deliverance Ministry. We must remember that an educated Christian (i.e., one who understands the nature of spiritual war and the strategy and tactics of the enemy) is a wise Christian. Romans 11:26 states:

> "And so all Israel shall be saved: as it is written, There shall come out of Zion the Deliverer, and shall turn away ungodliness from Jacob; for this is my covenant unto them, when I shall take away their sins."

Examing the practice of power encounters from the Old Testament through the New Testament established them in the context of the "Plan of God" to deliver His people. This plan of God is for the Church to embrace, understand, and utilize the practical ways that Jesus ministered healing and deliverance. This is not to suggest that these are formulas because there is no formula for deliverance. Jesus displayed His demonstrations of power as examples so that we, His followers, might recognize the manifestations and symptoms of demonized people and how they can be set free.

There is a broad range of viewpoints concerning Deliverance Ministry and spiritual warfare, so it is especially critical that Deliverance Ministry be based squarely on biblical principles. Thus, though there are no specific techniques that are universally applicable, there are spiritual principles in place that we must adhere to from the Word of God. Deliverance is divine and of God.

An overarching theme emerged in this study of deliverance—God's Love for His people is the motive for implementing His plan for deliverance. Buried deep inside of everyone is the need to be loved. Love is a very powerful weapon; demons despise love because God is love (1 John 4:8). Even when a person does not recognize or respond to love that is offered, pressure is applied in the spiritual realm, and demons are tormented when evil is confronted with the presence of agape Love.

Finally, we must accept the responsibility of the Church of Jesus Christ to move against the evil forces in an offensive manner (as discussed in the chapter on spiritual weapons). In order to do so, however, Christians must first defuse the fear that arises primarily out of ignorance, for what the Church does not understand, it fears. This is a natural response to lack of understanding, and thereby validates the intense need for a systematic Deliverance Ministry based on biblical principles and sound Church teachings and doctrine. God has shined a light on those in the Body who are willing to be used as instruments in destroying the plans of the enemy. When a believing Christian rises up against demons, with the authority of Jesus Christ and the power of the Holy Spirit and applies the shed blood of Jesus to any situation, the enemy and his demons must yield.

Deliverance Prayer

Prayers of deliverance are often prayed in the deliverance process as weapons. Proclaiming and declaring the Word of God torments the enemy. Here is an example of a prayer of deliverance making declarations, thanksgiving, confessions as well as proclaiming the Word of God:

> I pray to destroy every generational curse that may be at the root of my problem.
>
> I thank God because He is my source of deliverance.
>
> I thank God for His finished work on the cross of Calvary.
>
> I declare that my days of mourning are over.
>
> I boldly declare that I will not seek the Lord in vain.
>
> I declare that Christ has redeemed me from the curse of the law, having been made a curse for us.
>
> I cover myself with the blood of Jesus, as I break free from the power of demonic strongholds.
>
> I take authority over the power of darkness and command them to leave.
>
> I confess that I have been given power to forbid every work of the enemy.

I pronounce my deliverance from the demons of bitterness and resentment in the Name of Jesus.

I pronounce my deliverance from the demons of rebellion and disobedience in the Name of Jesus.

I pronounce my deliverance from the demons of strife, and bickering, in the Name of Jesus.

I pronounce my deliverance from the demons of control, dominance and possessiveness.

I pronounce my deliverance from fault-finding demons of criticism, accusation and judging.

I pronounce my deliverance from the demonic strongholds of self-rejection and the fear of rejection.

I pronounce my deliverance from the demons of inferiority, self-pity and inadequacy.

I break the control of the demons jealousy, envy and uncontrollable suspicion.

I pronounce myself free from the demons of depression, despair and discouragement.

I pronounce myself free from the demons of gloom, burden and heaviness.

I take authority over the demons of worry, anxiety and fear.

I pronounce myself free from the demon of nervousness, tension and headache.

I pronounce my freedom from the spirit of restlessness in the Name of Jesus.

I loose myself from the fear of man and the fear of disapproval, in the Name of Jesus.

I pray the Lord will turn every stone thrown at me by the enemy for my good.

I pronounce my deliverance from the demons of mental illness, of insanity in the Name of Jesus.

I take authority over the demons of paranoia and hallucination in the Name of Jesus.

I pronounce my deliverance from the demons of self-persecution, fear of condemnation and over-sensitivity, in the Name of Jesus.

I pronounce myself free from the paranoid tendencies of demonic envy, distrust and a confrontational spirit.

I pronounce myself free from the demons of frustration and forgetfulness, in the Name of Jesus.

I pronounce myself free from occult spirits and the practice of spiritism.

I pray the presence of the Lord will be magnified, even in the severest of battles.

I loose myself from the demon of egotism and pride, in the Name of Jesus.

I loose myself from the demons of binding fears.

I pronounce myself free from the demonic control of self-importance, self-righteousness and arrogance, in the Name of Jesus.

I pronounce myself free from impatience, frustration and criticism.

I pronounce myself free from the demons of grief, sadness and sorrow.

I pronounce myself free from the inexplicable tendencies toward tiredness, weariness and laziness.

I loose my freedom from the demons of infirmity, in the Name of Jesus.

I pronounce my freedom from demonic tendencies from generations past (physical, emotional, mental and curses), in the Name of Jesus.

I pronounce myself free from the demonic influence over my tongue,

Some examples are blasphemy, course jesting and gossip.

I pronounce myself free from the demonic spirits of criticism backbiting and mockery.

I pronounce myself free from bondage to addictive and compulsive substances.

I loose myself from the bondage of caffeine, alcohol, drugs, nicotine and gluttony.

I pronounce myself free from the demons of self-pity, frustration and resentment.

I pronounce myself free from the demons of shame and worthlessness in the Name of Jesus.

I loose myself from the demonic control of lust, fantasy lust, and masturbation.

I pronounce myself free from the demonic control of sensuality.

I pronounce myself free from the demons behind all occult practices, in the Name of Jesus.

I repent of the sins that have given demons the right of entry.

I pray to receive freedom from the demons of spiritism, in the Name of Jesus.

I cover my life with the blood, now that I am free, in the Name of Jesus.

I give praise to God, who always causes me to have victory.

I bless the Lord because no weapon formed against me will function.

I bless the Name of the Lord, because although the enemy may come against me one way, he will have to flee seven ways.

I thank the Lord because hope comes from Him to me.

I ask for forgiveness for whatever sins may have brought a curse on me.

I pray to reverse the curse of restlessness in my dwelling.

I pray to reverse every generational curse on my income, in Jesus' Name.

I pray to reverse every generational curse on my children, in Jesus' Name.

I pray to reverse every generational curse on my business in Jesus' Name.

I pray to reverse every curse placed on my labor in Jesus' Name.

I reject every curse of genetic disorder in my family, in the Name of Jesus.

I reject every curse of miscarriage and premature birth in my family, in the Name of Jesus.

I reject every curse pronounced on my journey, in the Name of Jesus.

I pray to reverse the curses of calamity, panic and frustration, in the Name of Jesus.

I pray to reverse the curse of incurable diseases, in the Name of the Lord.

I pray to reverse the curse of destructive diseases, such as incurable fever or skin conditions in the Name of Jesus.

I pray to reverse every curse that is causing unanswered prayer.

I reverse the curse of demonic infestation, in the Name of Jesus.

I pray to reverse the persistent presence of the demonic, in the Name of Jesus

AMEN

A Call to Arms

Deliverance Ministry is a very exciting and glorious life-changing ministry. My desire was to convey to the Christian community the importance of this ministry in the Church today. Considering the barrage of diabolical activities in the lives of the people of God, it is time to take into account the influence of the demonic realm. This ministry allows one to see the Bible actually come alive. There can be no true confession of being a Christian without being delivered from false doctrine into truth. This research was designed to encourage the Church to desire deliverance, first and foremost from error to truth. Error is false doctrine and gross darkness. Light is a metaphor for truth, and truth is the Gospel of Jesus Christ.

The Church cannot preach the Gospel and not activate and bring about deliverance; and it cannot preach deliverance without activating or affecting the Gospel. When Jesus came to the people He came as the "truth" with a ministry of deliverance. Truth brings about deliverance.

A caveat is in order. Though the Church cannot be close-minded it must be cautious in diagnosing and concluding that every situation or life-challenge or illness is demon-driven or of the devil. The research literature in the behavioral sciences reveals that some who were branded as demoniacs were in fact suffering from a mental disorder. There are many different diseases of the mind that are treated with medication that helps otherwise incapacitated people function and live active, fruitful lives. The precise relationship between various types of mental illness and demonic activity is beyond the scope of the present study. Suffice it to say here that this does not mean that demonic possession is not in existence in the form of psychosis, for, in fact, it is quite common. The decisive "diagnosis" has to be made, however, only after much counseling, dialogue, and discernment because of the delicate nature of the matter.

Ministers need experiential as well as spiritual and theological clarity in making an intelligent determination as to the presence of demonic activity that might coexist with a social or psychological problem. This is to reinforce the necessity of being fully knowledgeable as well as discerning of the signs and manifestations. This research is informative in regard to what is available to the Body of Christ and is intended to encourage the workers in Deliverance Ministry.

The theology of deliverance is very practical because it defines what salvation does to the believer, and deliverance defines what it means to be a Christian. By definition, salvation rescues one from the struggles of the enemy who is ever attempting to destroy him. Colossians 1:13 states:

*"Who hath delivered us from the power of darkness,
and hath translated us into the kingdom of His dear
Son."*

A true Christian is one who has been delivered from error to truth and understands truth. The truth must be proclaimed, preached, and taught in the Church in order to bring about deliverance. When the Church is helping the spiritually oppressed, it is engaging in a battle of spiritual forces of darkness. These dark forces are strategically sent out to prevent the Church from coming to the knowledge of truth. Through Deliverance Ministry the Body of Christ has the opportunity to witness the power of the Holy Spirit. He is the force that drives demons out and makes a deposit of Himself, which brings about great changes in the lives of God's people. This phenomenon testifies to the power and glory of God and brings the ministry of Jesus Christ to the forefront. This speaks volumes to the Body of Christ, to the world, and to the enemy, because in spite of what one may or may not think: "God is in Control."

Deliverance is a challenging ministry that can be quite discouraging at times. The price is great and the cost has to be counted. There is a definite risk of being hurt at the risk of being blessed; however, the blessing is worth the risk. It is the greatest of spiritual experiences to witness the very presence of the work of the Holy Spirit in deliverance. And the pinnacle of joy that spills over into the deepest places of the author's heart and soul makes an exhilarating deposit into my being. Oh, to be used by God. This is nothing done by human sources, for only God through the blood of Jesus has the power to bring victory over the devil in the life of His people. Faith, however, is the substance that brings the evidence of the power and authority of God. Deliverance is merely the evidence of the Word of God, through the power of the Holy Spirit. The Church has an obligation to embrace the whole "Deliverance Plan of God."

This is a ministry in which severe testing is always the order of the day. Please understand that in Deliverance Ministry there is no room for deliberate sins of the flesh. A higher standard of moral integrity should be emphasized in Christian leadership. God calls us to leadership because He requires more of us than He does of those we are called to lead. We are called to beyond reproach. Any aspirations we may have for Christian leadership requires a willingness to be made dead to the lusts of the flesh, self, and the pride of life (1 John 2:15-17). This is especially true of sins of any sexual nature. So much damage can be done when one opens oneself up to be sexually exploited by Satan. Indulging in fornication, adultery, or any type of bondage to sexual sins and attempting to minister deliverance is extremely risky. Within the Body of Christ, this is very potent poisonous venom used often to rapidly take down many men and women of God. Consequently, in Deliverance Ministers this area of sin has such potentially devastating consequences. It is wise to refrain from ministering if this is a problem until you have yourself been delivered and received victory over this problem. There is no sin worth ruining your ministry.

Spiritual warriors' greatest battles come not when they are engaged with demonic forces in someone being victimized, but when they are alone. We must be held accountable for our actions even when no one is watching. The life of Christian leaders—whether they are in the pulpit, platform, or in the privacy of their homes—is always under the watchful eye of the enemy. It is imperative to set one's face like a flint and never waiver. Paul gives the antidote; he simply says to run, escape, abscond, and avoid at all cost. In 2 Corinthians 6:18, he states:

*"Flee sexual immorality. Every sin that a man does is
outside the body, but he who commits sexual immorality sins against his own body."*

Moral integrity is the message here for ministering in deliverance. It is an admonition not to shame anyone—yourself, the pastor, the Church, the family, the community, and most of all our
Lord Jesus Christ. In going forth in ministry and in understanding and teaching Deliverance Ministry, let us always be mindful
of the critical importance of integrity. This is a big issue, and
there is no room for compromising in God's redemptive plan.
The plan is fool-proof; the commitment must be made to live up
to the standards set. The victory is in the obedience to bring God
glory and not shame. If obedience to the Word of God is not in
the heart of the Deliverance Minister, this is not the ministry to
pursue. We are called to live a moral life in the midst of an immoral society; we are not our own, we are called to be His ambas-
sadors on earth. Deliverance involves dictating to the forces of
darkness, and we know that Satan is a thug bent on stealing, killing, and destroying, and nothing would please him more than destroying the integrity of "God's Army of Warriors." This is a
charge to press on to the mark of the high calling, which is in
Christ Jesus.

Reflections

As I researched and wrote this book, I realized that deliverance is
one of the most difficult ministries in the Church today—not
only because of the controversial nature of deliverance but because of the perception in the world and in the Church of truth.
Everyone is looking for and actually wants the truth, but few are
experiencing it. Truth for me has become an experience, more

than words spoken and a belief system expressed. Truth is what we as Christians live in. This may sound like a cliché to those who have not yet come to the knowledge of the truth; however, truth is real. In fact, if we as Christians are not living in truth, we are being deceived and in fact living a lie. And it is as possible to live a lie as it is to live in truth. Through deception and clever manipulations, Satan has made it possible for mankind to first believe a lie, embrace it as though it is truth, live it, and ultimately become an opponent of the truth.

Many who were great evangelical contenders of the faith are now far from the truth. Did they ever experience the truth? My question along with the Apostle Paul, is who has bewitched the Church?

Galatians 3:1 states:

> *"O foolish Galatians, who hath bewitched you, that ye should not obey the truth, before whose eyes Jesus Christ has been evidently set forth, crucified among you?"*

Is it not the truth that still sets one free?

Hebrews 10:26 states:

> *"For if we sin willfully after that we have received the knowledge of the truth, there remaineth no more sacrifice for sins."*

It is my personal belief that the Church is experiencing the effects of Church without truth. What is truth? Jesus said that He Himself is the "the truth" in John 14:6:

> *"I am the way, the truth, and the life: no man cometh unto the Father, but by me."*

Where is the truth if not in the Church? John 16:13 states:

*"Howbeit when he, the Spirit of truth, is come, he
will guide you into all truth: for he shall not speak of
himself; but whatsoever he shall hear, that shall he
speak: and he will shew you things to come."*

Jesus said the "Spirit of Truth" will guide the Church into all truths. There is a need for the Church to come to the knowledge of truth and receive the Spirit of Truth. The Church should be full of the Holy Ghost. Deliverance is a ministry that requires the ministers of deliverance to be sanctified, disciplined, and patient. Deliverance Ministry must operate under a relationship with Jesus Christ that has been consummated and birthed out of a life of prayer. Prayer gives Christians an unquenchable thirst for the Word of God. Trying to minister deliverance without a relationship and a prayer life is playing with fire. When the opportunity to practice deliverance presents itself, it is difficult to remember all of the things that are taught in an occasional experience. Deliverance requires practice as well as extensive information to help the men and women of God to minister deliverance effectively.

This is not the time for the Church to be weak and powerless against a defeated enemy. Prayer enables believers are to walk in the supernatural. It is the means by which the Church is strengthened and unified. Prayer has been my greatest weapon during this time of constantly bombarding my mind with demonic literature and every immoral act of sin.

This ministry is not without consequences, which include many brutal attacks, physically, mentally, and spiritually from the enemy. These assaults can be against the Minister of Deliverance or of the family. The thought of invading the kingdom of darkness is as close to walking into the lion's den as one can get. The need to know that you know is applicable and what every Deliverance Minister must know is that "Jesus is Lord" over every aspect of a Christian's life.

My Prayer of Thanksgiving

I Thank God for Justifying and Sanctifying me by the Blood of Jesus.

I Thank God for His work for me on the Cross.

I Thank God because He is my Source of Deliverance.

I Thank God that my days of mourning are over.

I Thank God and I bow in worship and praise unreservedly to His majesty.

I Thank God for the blood of Jesus which is my protection and safe haven.

I Thank God that He forgives me and cleanses me of all my sins and unrighteousness.

I Thank God that He is my deliverer and Satan and his demons have no legal attachment me.

I Thank God for redeeming me from the filthiness of the devil, through the blood of Jesus.

I Thank God that all attempts to defile, bind, torment or harass me is nullified by the Blood.

I Thank God that Jesus is my deliverer and the only lover of my soul.

I Thank God that Jesus forgives me and places me in right standing with Him.

I Thank God that I am loosed from all demonic subjection, and set free in the Name of Jesus

I Thank God that I am able to renounce and rebuke satan, in the Name of Jesus.

I Thank God for sanctification and I close the door on all sins remembered and forgotten.

I Thank God all connections knowingly and unknowingly with the enemy are cancelled.

I Thank God all ties to the enemy are severed, cut, and broken, whether by word or deed.

I Thank God that my body is presented before Him as the temple of the Holy Ghost.

I Thank God that I can submit to God, resist the devil and he will flee from me.

I Thank God that He has not given me the spirit of fear but power, love, and sound mind.

I Thank God that the Truth, continually known by me shall keep me free.

I Thank God that I am strong in Him and in the power of His might.

I Thank God that I am able to stand, and having done all to stand, I can still stand..

I Thank God that I am dead to sin, but alive through Jesus Christ.

I Thank God I have peace with Him through Jesus Christ, by whom I have access by faith.

I Thank God as I humble myself before Him as a child before their Father.

I Thank God that I aspire to become a holy, loving, consecrated spirit before my Lord.

I Thank God that my foundation is buried in the absoluteness of your Holy Word.

I Thank God that my life and my strength is in His hand.

I Thank God that my will is to be available, with all diligence to His Will.

I Thank God that my existence is an expression of His Love for me.

I Thank God that His Word in me expresses grace and peace to a damaged soul.

I Thank God that I will always be as close as His breathed Word is in my heart.

I Thank God that my cry of deliverance is as close as His ear is to my prayer.

I Thank God for Jesus.

Glossary

IT IS IMPORTANT to understand the various terms used in this book. Use this section as a quick reference to the definition of terms related to deliverance ministry and spiritual warfare, as these words are used with connotations not conveyed in their common use in everyday language.

Abominations—idolatry, abhorrence, evil, curse, horror (e.g., in the scriptures homosexuality, lesbianism, and lying are considered abominations), uncleanness, perversions, obscenities, disgrace, witchcraft, pride, detestable and repugnant acts, persons, or things.

Affliction—physical or mental distress, anything causing suffering, pain, or calamity; affliction began with the Fall, when sin entered the world.

Addiction—compulsion, obsession, alcohol, drugs (illegal and prescription), nicotine, caffeine, sugar, exercise, spendthrift, food, craving. Addiction spirits lodge in the appetite, stomach, mouth, throat, taste buds, nose, mind, etc. They enter through rejection and inheritance.

Affinities—a natural attraction or inclination to a person or thing that is unholy.

Authority—the legal right to use power (from the koine Greek exousia, dunamis).

202 / I Declare War

Besetting Sin—sin that harasses persistently; habitual, soul-trying sin.

Blockage—obstruction; spirits that block spiritual growth, finances, relationships, prayer life, study of the Word, ministry, and other aspects of the abundant life of faith.

Bondage—slavery, subjection to restraint, servitude, yokes, chains, shackles, fetters, captivity.

Carnality—(Greek *sarkikos*) translates "rotten flesh", appetite of the soul, anti-spiritual, worldliness, lewdness, sensuality, lasciviousness, immorality.

Charmer—a hypnotist who charms the mind and will of another person to gain and exercise control over him or her.

Curses—Ancestral and generational, resulting from the "sins of the fathers." Refers also to the invocation of evil or injury against one's enemies; the opposite of blessing.

Cults—systems of religious worship, devotion to a person or thing other than the legitimate worship of God, practiced by such sects as Hare Krishna, Jehovah's Witnesses, Christian Science, and Mormonism; often use various mind-control tactics.

Death—separation from God (spiritual), cessation of life (physical).

Demons—disembodied spirits who take possession of human bodies; fallen angels who, under the leadership of Satan, rebel against God.

Devices—strategies, tactics, lines of attack, schemes, methods, plans, procedures.

Bitterness—unforgiveness, resentment, revenge, retaliation, root of bitterness (Hebrews 12:15), hidden bitterness, gall, poisonous root, hard bondage, murmuring, backbiting cursing, (opens the door for bodily sickness and infirmity).

Burdens—heaviness of spirit, heavy burdens, anxiety, albatross, hindrance, load, sorrow, stress, care, false burdens, guilt, oppression.

Divination—supposed insight into the future or unknown gained by supernatural means.

Doctrines of Devils/Demons—tradition, anti-Christ, divination, religion, idolatry.

Enchanter—one who casts spells upon people to control their actions.

Familiar Spirits—spirits that impersonate the dead, (spirit guides). These spirits are familiar with the family and go from generation to generation.

Fear—a reaction or phobia to something or someone that causes threat.

Hinder—block, stagnate, impede, and delay.

High Places—elevated places of worship.

Idolatry—the worship of idols marked by great adulation.

Leviathan—Pride, "king over all the children of pride" (Job 41:34). Sea monster, sea serpent, dragon; hardness of heart, vanity, conceit, ego, haughtiness, stubbornness. Operates through a curse (Psalm 119:21) and works with destruction (Proverbs 16:18).

Licentiousness—Debauchery, lewdness, nymphomania, concupiscence, lust, promiscuity, lawlessness, unrestraint.

Imaginations—the ability of the mind to be creative.

Occult—secretive, hidden, mysterious. Includes witchcraft, sorcery, divination, ESP, hypnosis, fortune-telling, consulting crystal ball, Ouija board, tarot cards; Freemasonry, martial arts, magic, séances, clairvoyance, mediums, psychics, readers, advisors, necromancy, handwriting analysis, astrology, yoga, metaphysical healing groups, hypnotism, occult movies, New Age movement, amulets, Transcendental Meditation, familiar spirits, (opens the door for multiple curses of sickness, death, destruction, confusion).

Obscenity—vulgarity, indecency, filthiness, shamelessness, vileness, licentiousness, immorality, uncleanness, lust, perversion, pornography, profanity, promiscuity.

Kingdom of Darkness—Satan's rule over diabolical entities, activities, principalities, and evil powers of this world.

Kingdom of Heaven—The sovereign rule of God, initiated by Christ's earthly ministry and consummated when the kingdom of the world becomes the kingdom of our Lord and Christ (Revelation 11:15).

Magic—the art of using hidden power.

Necromancer—one who supposedly communicates with the dead.

Observers of Times—a term used in the Bible to refer to astrology; one who observes the movements of the sun, moon, stars, and planets to predict the future of man.

Perversion—to turn from its proper use or nature

Power—the ability to do or act authorization, strength, energy.

Pride—vain, puffed-up, grand, flamboyant, arrogant, superior (spiritual or natural).

Princes—territorial powers that control certain nations, states, etc.

Principalities—a nation ruled by a prince with ruling authorities, territorial spirit.

Rebellion—open resistance to authority, anti-submissiveness, self-will, selfishness, self-deception, self-delusion, self-seduction, accusation, control, possessiveness, stubbornness, witchcraft.

Religious—the belief in a personal God; negatively, can manifest in doctrinal obsession, denominationalism, legalism, conservatism, dogmatic, tradition-bound, religious prejudice, divisiveness, false holiness, false tongues, self-righteousness, religious pride.

Rejection—refusal to accept or believe in, from mother, father, siblings; self-rejection; rejection from the womb, hurt, wounded, low self-esteem, bitterness, outcast, "black sheep."

Schism—division, contention, strife, denominational spirits, variance, pride, carnality.

Seducing Spirits—spirits that tempt, entice, or allure; as did Jezebel, Delilah.

Strife—contention, arguing, fighting, confusion, envy, discord, anger, bitterness, unforgiveness, competition, hatred.

Spirit of Suspicion—judgmental, conclusion drawn from what seems factual; by its nature causes disunity, distrust, fear, paranoia, doubt, hurt, accusation, rejection.

Stronghold—a fortified place, a secure refuge; manifested in high things, pride, imaginations, arguments, reasonings, disobedience, and rebellion.

Strongman—ruling spirit (Matthew 12:29); strongman of fear, rejection, rebellion, lust, infirmity, witchcraft, and so on.

Torment—physical or mental unrest, dis-ease.

Unclean Spirit—perverts the nature of man, directly associated with idolatry, witchcraft, and vileness.

Vexation—harassment, annoyance, irritation.

Wandering spirits—spirits that do not possess a body but exercise outward control, for example, through hypnosis and oppression that thus weaken their victims. They also direct mediums on what to say during séances.

Witch—a woman enchanter who has great demonic power.

Witchcraft—a religion that worships Satan and his demonic forces in order to receive magic power to influence the will of others through intimidation, manipulation, domination.

Wizard—one who uses magic or sorcery to control the will of others.

Yoke—dominion, servitude, a habit, a bond of union.

Voodoo—the use of or belief in witchcraft, skilled in sprinkling dust.

References & Reading

Anderson, Neil T., & Quarles, Mike & Julia. *Freedom From Addiction*. Ventura, CA: Regal Books: 1996.

Beck, James R., & Demarest, Bruce. *The Human Person in Theology and Psychology: Anthropology for the Twenty-First Century*. Kregel: 2005.

Bloomer, George G. *Weapons for Warriors*. Durham, NC: Blooming House Publishers: 2001.

Carson, D.A. *The Difficult Doctrine of the Love of God*. Wheaton, IL: Good News Publishers: 2000.

DeHaan, M.R. *The Chemistry of The Blood*. Grand Rapids, MI: Zondervan Publishing Company: 1943.

Duffield, Van Cleave. *Foudations of Pentecostal Theology*. San Dimas, CA: LIFE Bible College: 1983.

Williams, Duncan. *Binding the Strong Man*. South Bend, IN: Pneuma Life Publishing: 2002.

Elwell, Walter A. *Tyndale Bible Dictionary*. Wheaton, IL: Tyndale House Publishers: 2001.

Eckhardt, John. *Identifying and Breaking Curses*. New Kensington, PA: Whitaker House Publishers: 1999.

Eckhardt, John. *Deliverance Thesaurus: Demon Hit List*. New Kensington, PA: Whitaker House Publishers: 1995.

Ellis, Bill. *Raising the Devil*. Lexington, KY: The University Press of Kentucky: 2000.

Gibson, Noel & Phyl. *Evicting Demonic Intruders: Guidelines for Pastors and Counsellors on Ministering Freedom to the Oppressed*. Ventura, CA: Regal Books: 1993.

Gondwe, Eric. *Major Spiritual Warfare and Deliverance Ministry Principles*. JesusW.com and SpiritualWarfareDeliverance.com: Cambridge MA: 2006.

Horrobin, Peter J. *Healing Through Deliverance Volume 1*. Grand Rapids, MI: Chosen Books: 1991, 2003.

Horrobin, Peter J. *Healing Through Deliverance Volume 2*. Grand Rapids, MI: Chosen Books: 1991, 2003.

Ingram, Chip. *The Invisible War*. Grand Rapids, MI: Baker Books: 2006.

Lake, John G. *John G. Lake: His Life, His Sermons, His Boldness of Faith*. Fort Worth, TX: Kenneth Copeland Publications: 1994.

Larson, Bob. *Larson's Book of Spiritual Warfare*. Nashville, TN: Thomas Nelson Publishers: 1999.

Lockman Foundation. *MacArthur Study Bible*. Nashville, TN: Thomas Nelson Publishers: 2006.

Moody, D.L. *Secret Power*. New Kensington, PA: Whitaker House: 1997.

Murphy, Ed. *The Handbook for Spiritual Warfare*. Nashville,TN: Thomas Nelson Publishers: 2006.

Murray, Andrew. *The Blood of Christ*. Minneapolis, MN: Bethany House Publishers: 2001.

Nee, Watchman. *The Spiritual Man: Three Volumes*. New York, NY: Christian Fellowship Publishers: 1977.

Olukoya, D.K. *Overpowering Witchcraft*. Lagos, Nigeria: Mountain of Fire and Miracles Ministries Publications: 1999.

Pink, Arthur W. *The Attributes of God*. Wilder Publications: 2009.

Price, Paula. *The Prophet's Dictionary: The Ultimate Guide to Spiritual Warfare*. Apostolic Interconnect: 2002.

Prince, Derek. *Rules of Engagement*. Grand Rapids, MI: Chosen Books: 2006.

Prince, Derek. *Spiritual Warfare*. Springdale, PA: Whitaker House Publishers: 1987.

Rehmann, Scott & Elizabeth. *How to Minister Inner Healing and Deliverance*. Victoria, BC Canada: 2006.

Robeson, Jerry & Carol. *Strongman's His Name...What's His Game*. Woodburn, OR: Shiloh Publishing House: 1996.

Ross, Colin A. *Satanic Ritual Abuse: Principles of Treatment*. Toronto, ON: University of Toronto Press: 1995.

Savard, Liberty. *Shattering Your Strongholds*. New Brunswick, NJ: Bridge-Logos Publishers: 1998.

Spurgeon, Charles. *Prayer and Spiritual Warfare*. New Kensington, PA: Whitaker House Publishers: 1996.

Sumrall, Lester. *Demons: The Answer Book*. New Kensington, PA: Whitaker House Publishers: 2003.

Timmons, J.P. *Mysterious Secrets of the Dark Kingdom*. Austin, TX: CCI Publishing Company:1991.

Trimm, Cindy. *Rules of Engagement: Volume 2 Binding the Strong Man*. Ft. Lauderdale, FL: Kingdom Life Publishing: 2005.

Twerski, Abraham J. *From Pulpit…To Couch*. Pittsburgh: Mirkov Publications: 2005.

Twerski, Abraham J. *Addictive Thinking Understanding Self- Deception*. Center City MN: Hazelden: 1997.

Unger, Merrill F. *Biblical Demonology*. Grand Rapids, MI: Kregel Publications: 1994.

Vassal, Joy. *Demons Are Real*. Nashville, TN: Thomas Nelson Publishers: 2006.

Warner, Timothy M. *Spiritual Warfare*. Wheaton, IL: Good News Publishers: 1991.

Whyte, H.A. Maxwell. *Demons & Deliverance*. New Kensington, PA: Whitaker House Publishers: 1989.

Zondervan. *Life Application Bible*. Wheaton, IL: Tyndale House Publishers: 1991.

DR. DEBORAH W. NELSON is a widow after 28 years of marriage, and a retired Communications Technician after 30 years of service. The mother of two daughters and four beautiful grand-daughters. Dr. Nelson was saved in 1993, and called into ministry in 1997 at which time she started her studies at the National Bible College. Dr. Deborah Nelson's vision is to minister both nationally and internationally enhancing the lives of the people of God through an empowering ministry of missionary servants. This led to the birth of the "International Alliance Ministry of Servants (IAM'S)."

Dr. Nelson is the Founder, President and Senior Servant of IAM'S a ministry of servants called and committed to the mission fields of the world, IAM'S was established and incorporated in 2006, and as a result has formed Missionary Teams and traveled to Kenya, East Africa, to empower Bishops, Pastors, men, women and orphaned children in the Village of Taita Hills, Ngambwa and Mombasa. The work of the ministry is IAM'S, however the results of the mission belong to the Lord God. The love and commitment to building an orphanage for 150 children in Taita Hills, the feeding and clothing of the orphans is the ministry of IAM'S by the love and grace of God.

Dr. Nelson is on the faculty of National Bible College / Seminary, and has earned her Doctoral Degree of Ministry in June 2009, Master of Divinity in June 2005, Master of Theological Studies in June 2003, Bachelor of Theology in May 2001, Associate of Theological Studies in May of 1999, Ministerial Internship Program Certificate in May of 1998 from the National Bible College / Seminary located in Ft. Washington, MD.

Breinigsville, PA USA
18 March 2010
234373BV00001B/5/P